THE ROUTLEDGE
ATLAS
OF
AFRICAN AMERICAN
HISTORY

Routledge Atlases of American History

Series Editor: Mark C. Carnes

The Routledge Historical Atlas of the American Railroads
John F. Stover

The Routledge Historical Atlas of the American South
Andrew K. Frank

The Routledge Historical Atlas of Women in America
Sandra Opdycke

THE ROUTLEDGE

ATLAS

OF

AFRICAN AMERICAN

HISTORY

JONATHAN EARLE

MARK C. CARNES, SERIES EDITOR

ROUTLEDGE

NEW YORK AND LONDON

Published in 2000 by
Routledge
29 West 35th Street
New York, NY 10001

Published in Great Britain in 2000 by
Routledge
11 New Fetter Lane
London EC4P 4EF

Printed in the United Kingdom on acid-free paper.

10 9 8 7 6 5 4 3 2 1

Library of Congress Cataloging-in-Publication Data

Earle, Jonathan
The Routledge atlas of African American history / Jonathan Earle.
p. cm. -- (Routledge atlases of American history)
Includes bibliographical references and index.
ISBN 0-415-92136-8 (acid-free paper) -- ISBN 0-415-92142-2 (pbk. : acid-free paper)
1. Afro-Americans--History. 2. Afro-Americans--History--Maps. I. Title: Atlas of African American history. II. Title. III. Series.

E185 .E125 2000
973'.0496073--dc21 99-059713

For James Patrick Shenton,

who taught me to love history.

Contents

Foreword

Slavery is the central—arguably the defining—dilemma of the American nation, the first large experiment in democracy. Democracy presumes equality—why else tot up votes to determine a majority?—but from its inception, the American nation countenanced a slave system that defined some human beings as less than human. "That all men are created equal," Thomas Jefferson wrote in the Declaration of Independence, was a "self-evident" truth. Yet he justified owning human beings, degrading them, and exploiting their labor on the grounds that African Americans were "inferior to whites in the endowments both of body and mind."

Slavery and its repercussions are central to this volume, the fourth in the Routledge Atlases of American History. In this atlas Jonathan Earle, a history professor at the University of Kansas, author of *The Undaunted Democracy: Jacksonian Antislavery and Free Soil: 1824–1854*, seeks to show—to demonstrate visually—that slavery was not merely a constellation of ideas, but a cultural institution that left a deep imprint, literally and figuratively, upon the American nation.

Thus the earliest maps in the atlas focus on Africa, where a slave trade antedated the arrival of Portuguese traders in West Africa in the 15th century. The atlas emphasizes the economic forces that caused hundreds of thousands of Africans to be shipped to the Americas, where legal and political arrangements were devised to perpetuate their subjugation.

Earle shows how the slave system in the South matured along the Atlantic seaboard, and then spread westward with the diffusion of cotton cultivation in the early 19th century. This social migration transformed American politics as well, resulting in the fateful stalemate that led to the Civil War. After delineating the slave system in its entirety, Earle looks at the phenomenon close up: from the vantage point of a slave dwelling in one set of maps; from the perspective of a single plantation in another. Earle considers as well the aftermath of slavery, ranging from post-Civil War Reconstruction to Rosa Parks and the Montgomery Bus Boycott nearly a century later.

Slavery was indisputably harsh and degrading; but Earle sides with scholars who contend that slaves were not powerless victims. He examines in gripping detail instances where African Americans defied the slave system: the Stono Revolt in 18th-century South Carolina, Nat Turner's Rebellion in 19th-century Virginia, the flight of thousands of runaway slaves, the exploits of African Americans who fought in the Union Army. Liberation came decades earlier for slaves in the North, where there emerged a distinctive African-American culture, expressed through African-American churches, newspapers, and other unique cultural institutions.

Thus while slavery was central to the evolution of this nation, and to the experiences of African Americans, it did not define those experiences. The history of African Americans is not the history of American slavery: it is something far greater. Earle's special challenge has been to delineate this larger realm of experience.

To that end, he has explored many topics that are commonly overlooked: Marcus Garvey's attempts to repatriate African Americans to Africa, the major role of African-American soldiers in 20th-century wars; the evolution of the Negro Baseball Leagues; the rise of the Nation of Islam; the emergence of the Harlem literary Renaissance; the birth of jazz.

This is a large and complex story: Earle tells it by joining a wealth of information, conveyed through maps, graphs, tables, and pictures, with a concise and authoritative narrative. This atlas will prove indispensable to educators and scholars, and absorbing to those interested in coming to terms with this nation's past, and with its destiny.

Mark C. Carnes
Professor of History
Barnard College, Columbia University

Introduction

> Hither too came the Negro. From the first he was the concrete test of that search for Truth, of the strife toward a God, of that body of belief which is the essence of true religion. His presence rent and tore and tried the souls of men.
> —W. E. B. DuBois, 1924

This small volume strives to tell, with maps, the story of the peoples of African descent in America. The story is a complex one that could easily fill the pages of a dozen atlases, monographs, and textbooks. Instead of attempting to be encyclopedic, then, I tried to focus on elements of African American history that could be enhanced with maps. When executed well and supported with appropriate text, images, and tables, maps can make history more understandable and—in the best circumstances—bring people's stories to life. This is precisely what I have attempted here.

With this in mind, the atlas begins centuries before the arrival of Africans in North America. The first part, "The Roots of Black America," begins by documenting the rich and varied history of African peoples, including the mighty kingdoms of Mali and Songhay. Other maps trace the progression of both the internal African and trans-Atlantic slave trades, which scattered millions of Africans across the globe to toil for others. In the New World, these African immigrants encountered societies in rapid transformation. During the 50 years after the first Africans arrived in Virginia, for example, blacks witnessed their status as unfree laborers (a condition shared by numerous others, including white indentured servants) deteriorate into one of life servitude for themselves and their offspring. Maps illustrate how these mostly African-born blacks developed their own cultures of work, belief, family, and identity. A map of the Stono slave revolt of 1739 shows that slaves did not watch passively as the slave system solidified around them. Stono and the resulting murder of the rebellious slaves starkly demonstrated the growing fear among whites—especially in black-majority colonies like South Carolina—that slaves might rise as one to throw off their chains and seek vengeance. A final map functions as a snapshot of the black population on the eve of the American Revolution, at a time when American-born blacks (or Creoles) had begun to emerge as a dominant force in the community. Unlike slave communities in the Caribbean or in the early years of North American settlement, the slave population in what would soon become the United States began an uninterrupted process of natural increase. This attribute would become extremely significant during the early history of the American republic.

The second part, "Two Communities, Slave and Free," focuses on the years of the new American nation when two black communities—separate but forever linked by heritage, family, and oppression—developed and flourished. Following recent scholarship, the maps attempt to show a people forging a new culture, one rooted squarely in the African past but also incorporating strong American elements. Free blacks, increasingly concentrated in the Northern states, struggled for rights granted to whites and founded institutions to help stem a rising tide of racism. Maps focus specifically on two of these institutions: the African Methodist Episcopal Church and the black press. Other maps document the abolition of slavery in the North and, in what at first seems like a contradiction, the rise of legal discrimination there. In the South, where slavery became immensely profitable and expanded rapidly into new Western lands, enslaved blacks developed their own religion, traditions, and culture to endure the hardships of thralldom. Four diverse maps illustrate the economy of plantation slavery, and two others focus on slave life, both in the fields and in the quarters. Finally, a detailed map of Southampton County, Virginia, documents the slave rebellion led by Nat Turner. Turner and his band murdered every white person they could find over two nights in 1831, striking a powerful—and bloody—blow for freedom.

"Toward Freedom," the third part, follows African American resistance to slavery through its destruction during the Civil War. One map illustrates how free blacks and their white allies helped build a loosely organized but effective "Underground Railroad" to assist slaves escaping northward, often with the help of "conductors" like the ex-slave Harriet Tubman. Another map details the escape routes taken by several runaway slaves like Frederick Douglass, who became the most famous black orator and author of his day, and William and Ellen Craft, who escaped from Georgia by impersonating a white slaveholder and her trusted servant. Success stories like Douglass's and the Crafts' were rare, however, so the same map also includes the route used to return apprehended fugitive Anthony Burns to slavery and the harrowing journey of the kidnap victim Solomon Northrup, who spent 12 years as a slave before returning home to New York. Maps in this part also detail how attempts to "compromise" over the issue of slavery and its expansion failed—repeatedly—between 1819 and 1857, leading to the Civil War. Once the war started, the escape to Union camps by thousands of runaway slaves (called "contrabands") forced Union leaders to see the possibilities of a war for freedom and forced Abraham Lincoln to issue the Emancipation Proclamation. After the war ended, freed slaves in the South won civil and political rights, and a map illustrates the first elected black officials during Reconstruction. Such victories were fleeting, however, and Reconstruction ended when Union troops ended their occupation in 1877. Soon thereafter,

Born a slave in Maryland, Frederick Douglass became one of the leading figures in African American history. A brilliant speaker and writer, he worked tirelessly for the abolition of slavery, equal justice for blacks, and universal human rights abroad.

facing intimidation, violence, and murder, the first significant wave of African American migrants left the South to found all-black towns in Kansas, Oklahoma, and California.

Part Four, "African Americans Under Arms," temporarily breaks the atlas' chronological organization and traces black participation in the military from the Revolution through recent action in Haiti and the Balkans. Since colonial times, blacks have volunteered for service believing that military action during wartime was a path to greater freedom and opportunity for themselves and their people. At no time was this belief more widely held than during the Civil War, when thousands of African Americans volunteered to combat slavery and the Confederacy by fighting in the Union Army. Frederick Douglass called the decision to use black troops—forbidden before 1863—a "golden opportunity . . . [for blacks to] win for ourselves the gratitude of our country, and the blessings of our posterity through all time." Black valor and courage among soldiers in units like the 54th Massachusetts helped to destroy slavery and the Confederacy, but failed to translate into better treatment for African Americans in the military and in the larger society. This pattern was evident in military actions over the next 130 years: blacks joined up to prove their mettle in battle and to open new paths of opportunity after the shooting stopped; yet time after time black soldiers mustered out only to encounter racism and bitter disappointment. Several maps in this part detail the use of African American soldiers during the era of the segregated armed forces, including the Buffalo Soldiers, the Spanish-American War, and World Wars I and II. After 1948, when President Truman desegregated all U.S. armed forces, blacks served alongside whites both in battle and in peacetime. Additional maps illustrate black soldiers' involvement in conflicts in Korea, Vietnam, and the Persian Gulf and in peacekeeping missions in Somalia and Haiti. Although great strides toward racial equality have been made in the integrated military, African

Blacks lobbied hard for the right to fight against the Confederacy in the Civil War. On July 18, 1863 the 54th Massachusetts Infantry, the first black regiment raised in the North, led a courageous and bloody assault on Fort Wagner, part of the network of defenses surrounding Charleston, SC.

Americans still cite numerous examples of racism and racist behavior as impediments to their advancement.

Part Five, "The Struggle for Equality," takes up where Part Three left off—with the use of terror and murder to intimidate African Americans and trample their constitutional rights. Maps detail the disfranchisement of black voters and the systematic enactment of racist laws (called "Jim Crow" laws) to separate the races. One prominent scholar called the period after Reconstruction "the nadir" of American race relations, yet it was also a time of building and achievement. Maps illustrate the founding of hundreds of black colleges and universities and the stunning success of segregated Negro Leagues baseball. Another map revisits the Great Migration of blacks to Northern and Midwestern cities. The chapter then shifts focus to the civil rights movement and the destruction of Jim Crow, with maps focusing on the Montgomery bus boycott, the rise of the sit-in movement, and the struggle for voting rights. A final map links African decolonization in the 1950s and '60s with the rise of black nationalism, an ideology pioneered in the 19th century and perfected by Marcus Garvey in the 1920s and Malcolm X in the 1960s.

The final part, "The African American Community," again breaks out of the chronological structure. The chapter initially focuses on the formation of a distinct African American culture in the 20th century and its impact on American culture as a whole. A map of the Harlem Renaissance details the block-by-block growth of the "black Mecca" in the 1920s, and demonstrates the cultural influences of authors like Zora Neale Hurston, poets like Langston Hughes, political leaders like Marcus Garvey, and institutions like the Apollo Theater on 125th Street. The literary voices of Harlem had a tremendous impact on the world of letters, just as the "voices" of jazz and blues greats like Louis Armstrong and Robert Johnson profoundly affected the world of music. The black musical tradition also includes the development of genres like rock 'n' roll, soul, and hip hop. Another map attempts to illustrate the diverse origins of African American intellectuals, writers, musicians, and entertainers. The remaining maps in the section detail recent political and demographic changes in the African American community. One focuses on the realignment of black voters from reliable Republicans to die-hard Democrats in the 1920s and 1930s. Another details the urbanization of the black community and spotlights the election of African American mayors. A final map features a snapshot of the African American community as recorded by the 1990 U.S. Census. That study revealed an African American community that continues to be mobile, complex, and influential.

No atlas can present a finished representation of a people, especially one as varied and diverse as Americans of African descent. Experts and amateurs alike will no doubt uncover errors, omissions, and arguments with which they passionately disagree. Yet I hope the picture of the American experience presented here—using maps to tell African Americans' stories—reveals to each interested reader something about a moving and fascinating history.

PART I: THE ROOTS OF BLACK AMERICA

> The first object which saluted my eyes when I arrived on the [West African] coast was the sea, and a slave ship which was then riding at anchor and waiting for its cargo . . . I was soon put down under the decks, and there I received such a salutation in my nostrils as I had never experienced in my life: so that I was not able to eat . . . but soon, to my grief, two of the white men offered me eatables, and on my refusing to eat, one of them held me fast and laid me across the windlass, and tied my feet while the other flogged me severely.
> —Olaudah Equiano, 1756

In 1619, 20 black people splashed ashore at Jamestown in the British colony of Virginia. A Dutch captain had brought them from Africa and sold them to the English colonists in exchange for water and supplies. The arrival of these Africans was a momentous event in American history, even if it was only briefly noted by Jamestown's leader: human beings from three continents—Africa, Europe, and America—together occupied a ribbon of land on the southeastern coast of North America. Their futures would be intertwined forever after.

Historians cannot answer even the most basic questions about these first black inhabitants of North America. What were their ethnic backgrounds? What was their legal status? How many were men? Women? The Englishman left these important details out of his journal. But one thing is certain: there was more on board that Dutch frigate than human cargo. The people disembarking brought with them the diverse social, linguistic, economic, religious, and political traditions from their African homeland. It was a homeland that was likely the birthplace of humankind—excavations in the Olduvai Gorge in northern Tanzania suggest that hominids began using tools there about 2 million years ago. More than that, it was a homeland that witnessed the emergence and development of vast civilizations, sophisticated cultures, and diverse peoples. Over time, the descendants of those first humans created literally hundreds of separate cultures in Africa. Those cultures varied as widely as the continent's geography. More important, many of these various cultures remained in substantial contact with each other, adding to the diversity. Anthropologists and linguists estimate that modern Africa contains more than 800 linguistic and ethnic groups, each with its own unique culture and religion.

This substantial African past was transported across the Atlantic along with the people aboard that Dutch ship and the thousands that followed. What's more, scholars like Carter G. Woodson, John Blassingame, and Albert Raboteau have demonstrated that this African cultural heritage continues to influence American (not just African American) life to this day. It survives in contemporary American religion; in folk tales told to children; in English words like *banjo*, *yam*, and *canoe*; and in the way we work, play, and congregate socially.

Finally, there was something unique about the Africans who came to America. It was not their status as unfree laborers: thousands of Europeans crossed the Atlantic as indentured servants and bound laborers, and the labor of Native Americans was similarly coerced in the New World. And as this section points out, slavery and the slave trade existed in Africa before Europeans arrived with their ships in the 15th century. The Africans in the New World were unique because, with very few exceptions, they did not choose to make the trip. The African dispersion was thus forced on unwilling emigrants who, as the 17th century wore on, were legally defined as chattel and denied basic rights. This, as much as their shared African heritage, influenced the formation of African Americans as a people.

For the first hundred years after the arrival of those first Africans at Jamestown, African-born people dominated the emerging slave society in colonial British America. But by the mid-18th century, American-born blacks were forging a new culture, one that combined the African heritage of their ancestors with the New World in which they were born. This process was by no means smooth or easy: at times, as with the Stono rebellion of 1739, it was outright brutal. But by the 1760s these "new" people had laid the foundations of black America.

Slaves at work on a tobacco farm in Virginia. Tobacco production involved indentured servants and slaves in a complex and specialized work process as they planted, cut, cured, stripped, and packaged the leaf for export.

The African Past

The Empires of Africa, 900–1500

African societies developed a large variety of political systems, ranging from loosely structured groups to immense and powerful empires. Anthropologists date the emergence of states in the Nile River valley to about 3500 B.C. Of these ancient societies, Egypt was the most significant. Ancient Egypt's contributions to African, European, and Middle Eastern cultures are well known, especially in such areas as hieroglyphic writing, mathematics, and geography. During the medieval period, the empires of Morocco (controlled by Muslim people called Almoravids), Algiers (controlled by the Almohads), and Egypt (controlled by the Fatimids) dominated the lands of the Mediterranean in both Africa and Europe. Key to their ability to dominate North Africa was their common religion—Islam—which led to lucrative military and trade alliances.

Most African Americans trace their ancestry to West Africa, where numerous powerful and wealthy civilizations rose and fell between the 9th and 16th centuries. The earliest of these was the kingdom of Ghana, located along the grasslands of the Senegal and upper Niger rivers. Records before 900 are sketchy, but by that time Ghana was well known for its fabulous wealth and powerful army. Its economic strength was derived from its vast supplies of gold and participation in an active trans-Saharan trade in items like salt and copper. Ghanaian scholars made advances in mathematics and astronomy, and, at the kingdom's peak in the 11th century, its leaders commanded an army of 20,000 soldiers. In 1076 Muslim Almoravids invaded Ghana, seized the capital, and made it an Islamic city. The conflicts that resulted undermined the kingdom, and it collapsed around 1200.

In its place arose the even more powerful empire of Mali, one of the world's richest and most advanced civilizations. By the early 1300s, Mali extended more than 1,000 miles inland from its border on the Atlantic Ocean, covering much of what is now francophone Africa. Travelers' accounts focus on the kingdom's prosperity, order, sophistication, and Muslim piety. When Mali's king made a pilgrimage to Mecca in 1324, his entourage—which consisted of more than 8,000 retainers, 500 slaves, and 100 camels each carrying 300 pounds of gold—sent Cairo's economy into an inflationary spiral. ("So much gold was current in Cairo that it ruined the value of money.")

In 1468 Mali was conquered by the kingdom of Songhay, which dominated West Africa for more than 300 years. The empire's greatest legacy was the system of universities in Timbuktu, Gao, Walata, and Jenne, which attracted scholars from all over Africa, Europe, and Asia. During this period several smaller West African kingdoms of note rose and fell, including Dahomey, Kanem, Benin, Wolof, Senegambia, and Asante.

Nubia and Ethiopia in East Africa provided vital links with the Mediterranean and the Middle East, and were among the first African nations to convert to Christianity. City-states and smaller nations dotted the east coast of Africa, including Somalia, Tanganyika, Katanga, and Zanzibar. What is

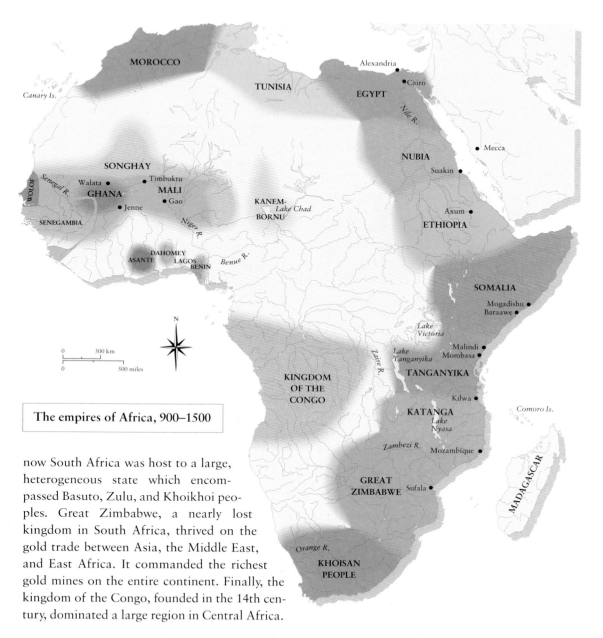

| The empires of Africa, 900–1500 |

now South Africa was host to a large, heterogeneous state which encompassed Basuto, Zulu, and Khoikhoi peoples. Great Zimbabwe, a nearly lost kingdom in South Africa, thrived on the gold trade between Asia, the Middle East, and East Africa. It commanded the richest gold mines on the entire continent. Finally, the kingdom of the Congo, founded in the 14th century, dominated a large region in Central Africa.

The Trans-Saharan Slave Trade, 900–1500

Even before the rise of Islam in the 7th century, North African Berbers used their knowledge of the Sahara Desert's geography to control several lucrative trade routes from northern Africa and southern Europe to West Africa. This elaborate network of trade routes helped initiate the world's first "global" economy by connecting West Africa, the Mediterranean, the Middle East, and

Asia. There was considerable demand in the West African kingdoms of Ghana, Mali, and Songhay for silk, cotton, beads, salt, mirrors, and dates; in return they provided traders with gold, kola nuts, ivory, and slaves. Slaves eventually equaled and then surpassed gold as West Africa's major export.

Slavery thus had a long history on the continent before Europeans arrived in sub-Saharan Africa in the 15th century, but in a form far less brutal than the type the Europeans would impose. Slavery played a prominent part in ancient civilizations like Egypt, Greece, and Rome, where slaves were either captured or purchased to perform menial tasks. Invading Muslims would typically capture African men for military service and personal servants, and women for their harems. It was not uncommon to find black slaves in places like Persia or

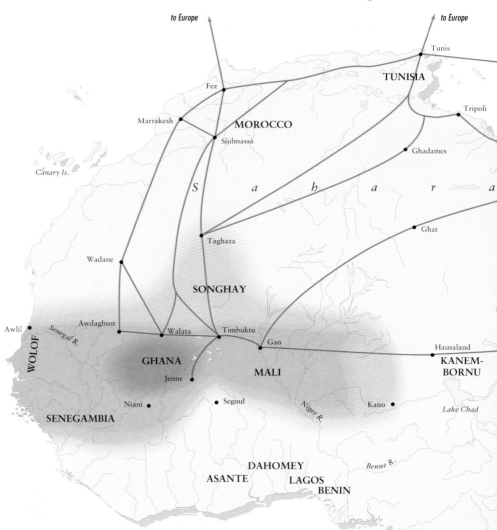

Arabia. As political leaders in West Africa converted to Islam, they often cooperated in the trade of (mostly non-Muslim) slaves.

There is little doubt that this form of African slavery was cruel and exploitative, but it had several differences from the later slave system. First, slavery had no definitive racial basis, and slaves were not isolated as a separate caste. Slaves could be whites from southern Europe, Middle Eastern people, or black Africans. Second, slaves primarily worked as servants for their owners—not as endlessly toiling agricultural laborers whose production of staple crops served to enrich slaveholders. Since there were no large-scale cotton or sugar plantations in the Muslim world, the harshness and permanent exploitation that characterized New World slavery was less apparent. Third, slavery was not always a permanent and inherited status. All of these things changed when Portuguese ships arrived on the coast of West Africa in the 15th century.

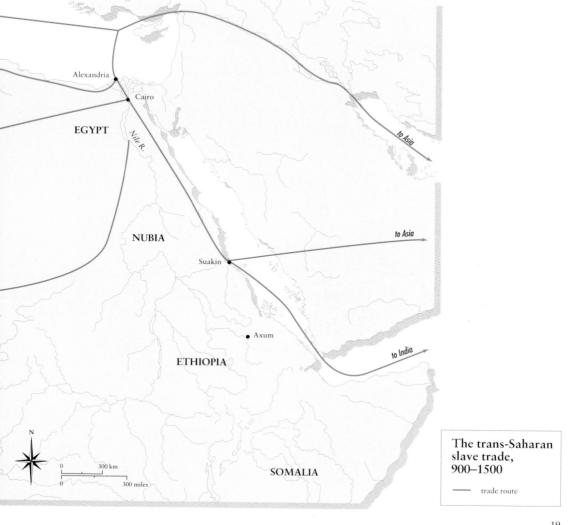

The trans-Saharan
slave trade,
900–1500

—— trade route

The Trans-Atlantic Slave Trade, 1500–1800

Slave Trade in Africa, 1750

After an enslaved captive was purchased by slave traders on the African coast, the purchaser's insignia was branded onto the slave's shoulder, breast, or buttocks.

Right: Located on the Gold Coast of West Africa, Cape Coast Castle was one of the leading slave-trading forts between the 16th and 19th centuries. Slaves were housed in forts like these—often in cramped, subterranean dungeons— before being loaded onto ships for the dreaded passage across the Atlantic.

By the end of the 15th century, Europeans had superceded their Arab and African counterparts and established a modern, trans-Atlantic slave trade. A commercial revolution in Europe led to the rise of powerful nation-states like Portugal, Spain, Britain, France, and Holland, as well as new ideas about competition, commodity exploitation, and the accumulation of wealth. The importing and exporting of African slaves became an accepted and profitable part of European commerce.

Portugal was the first European nation to see the economic advantages of the African slave trade. The Portuguese made the slave trade possible by exploiting rivalries among the more than 200 small states and ethnic groups of West and Central Africa. Despite their cultural similarities, West Africans neither viewed themselves as a single people nor shared a universal religion that might have restrained them from selling other Africans into slavery. Christian Europeans who believed that enslaving fellow Christians was immoral had few moral qualms about enslaving pagan or Muslim Africans.

As early as 1502, Portuguese traders were shipping West African slaves to Spanish and Portuguese colonies in the Caribbean and Brazil to work on sugar plantations. As West Indian plantations grew in size and economic importance, the slave trade mushroomed, employing thousands of persons, involving millions of dollars of capital, and beginning the largest forced migration in history. Almost immediately, Europeans (first the Portuguese, then the French, English, Dutch, Swedes, and others) began to build an extensive network of forts along the African coast. The Gold Coast, which became contemporary Ghana, contained more than 50 of these forts along its 300-mile coast on the Gulf of Guinea, including Elmina Castle (the oldest, built by the Portuguese in 1482) and Cape Coast Castle (built by the Swedes in 1653, but later captured by the British). Cape Coast Castle could hold up to 1,500 slaves in its dark, damp dungeons at the peak of the trans-Atlantic slave trade. The forts were constructed with the permission of local rulers, who were paid rent. They also had to be defended against constant assaults from rival Europeans and Africans.

The enslaved Africans lost their liberty in a variety of ways. Wars between African states provided many of the captives who fueled the slave trade (one authority claims that as many as 80 percent of slaves were prisoners of war and came from a state other than that of the seller). Other slaves had been deprived of their civil rights after being convicted of a crime. Still others were kidnap victims, although kidnappers faced severe penalties if caught. Debtors, orphans, and people who lacked kinship ties with other members of their state made up the rest of those sold to slave traders.

African traders usually marched their slaves to the coastal forts in chains, in groups of up to 150 people. Once on the coast, purchasers were allowed to examine the slaves' stature, teeth, limbs, and genitals before deciding whether or not to buy. After purchase the slave's skin was branded with the insignia of

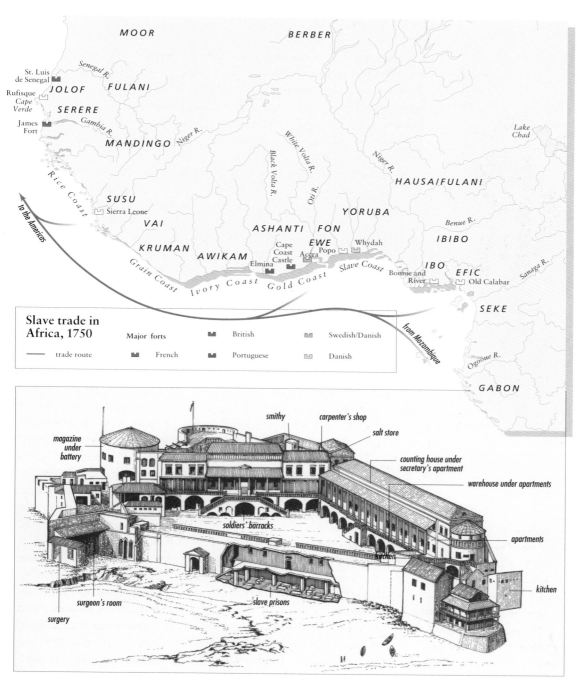

MOOR

BERBER

St. Luis
de Senegal

Senegal R.

JOLOF   FULANI

Rufisque
Cape
Verde

SERERE

James
Fort

Gambia R.

MANDINGO   *Niger R.*

White Volta R.

Black Volta R.

Oti R.

Niger R.

Lake
Chad

HAUSA/FULANI

Rice Coast

to the Americas

SUSU

Sierra Leone

VAI

KRUMAN   AWIKAM

Grain Coast   *Ivory Coast*   *Gold Coast*

ASHANTI   FON

Cape
Coast
Castle   EWE   Popo   Whydah

Elmina   Accra

Slave Coast

YORUBA

Benue R.

IBIBO

IBO   EFIC

Bonnie and
River   Old Calabar

Sanaga R.

SEKE

from Mozambique

Ogooue R.

GABON

Slave trade in Africa, 1750

Major forts	British	Swedish/Danish
⎯ trade route	French	Portuguese	Danish

smithy   carpenter's shop

salt store

magazine
under
battery

counting house under
secretary's apartment

warehouse under apartments

soldiers' barracks

apartments

kitchen

surgeon's room

slave prisons

kitchen

surgery

his or her purchaser. The branded slave then waited, often in subterranean dungeons, for their ships to depart for the Americas. Many died waiting.

The Africans who were brought to the North American mainland (often after spending time in the Caribbean) originated in an area bounded by the

After arriving in the Americas, enslaved Africans were sold at auction. By the mid-18th century slavery was well entrenched in all 13 British colonies in North America.

Senegal River in the north and Angola in the south. Principal ethnic groups inhabiting this area included the Yoruba, Fon, and Ibo peoples from the Bight of Biafra; the Ashanti and other Akan-speaking people from the Gold Coast; the Susu from Sierra Leone; and the Jolof, Serere, Mandingo, and Fulani from the Senegambia. Slaves from the Bakongo, Tio, and Mbundu groups from the Congo-Angola region were also brought to North America.

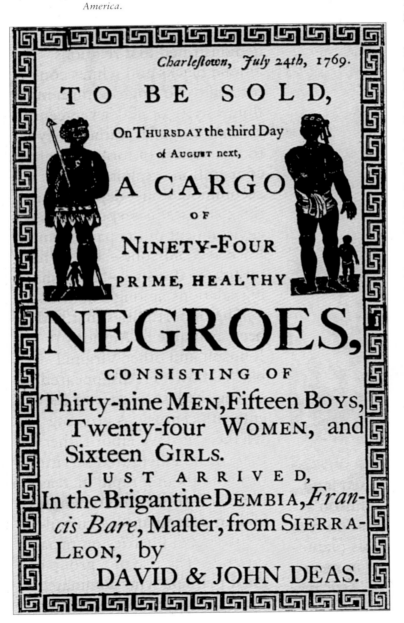

Destinations of African Slaves

For those who survived the cramped and dangerous confinement on the coast, the nightmare was only beginning. The one-way trip to the Americas was known as the "Middle Passage." Slaves were chained together by twos at their hands and feet, and stacked as tightly as possible in the ship's hold, "like books on a shelf." Since more cargo meant more profit, the slaves were denied standing, lying, or even sitting room. This routine practice of overcrowding led to disastrous outbreaks of disease during the voyage, which lasted from 6 to 16 weeks. Smallpox, dysentery, and various other fevers and fluxes passed quickly from person to person; modern scholars estimate the mortality rate on the ships averaged between 25 and 40 percent during the early years of the slave trade.

Traders learned very quickly to keep slaves securely chained for the duration of the voyage. Given the opportunity, many unchained slaves chose suicide over a lifetime of enslavement in the Americas. Moreover violent rebellions by slaves occurred frequently enough to keep fear in the hearts of even experienced traders. As plantations and populations in the Americas grew in size and economic importance, so too did the slave trade. As the map illustrates, most slaves departing Africa did not go to North America: a slave was almost ten times as likely to wind up in the West Indies as he was to land in the United States. After Caribbean islands like Santo Domingo and Cuba, Brazil was the most likely destination.

Between 1619 and 1808, when Congress abolished the slave trade, nearly 400,000 Africans were brought against their will to British North America and the United States. Approximately 8 million more were taken to the sugar and coffee plantations in Brazil and the Caribbean or to the mines of Spanish America.

Destinations of African slaves

- area of origin of slaves
- area of slave settlement
- slave shipping, with numbers in thousands

Major port of embarkation

- French
- British
- Portuguese
- Swedish/Danish

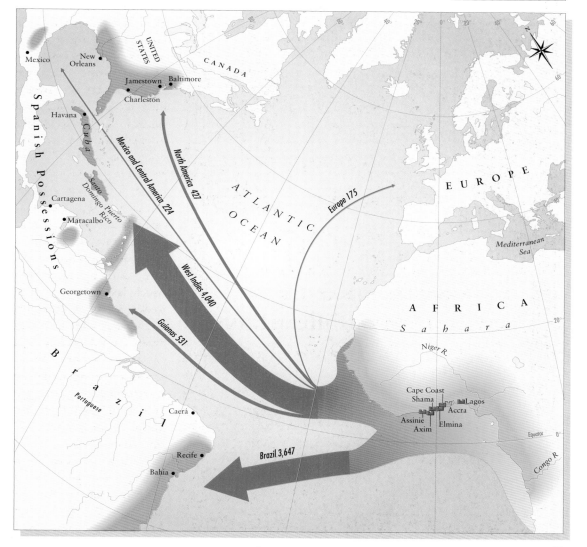

The African Dispersion

An estimated 9 million Africans were taken from their homeland aboard European ships like the one in this wood cut, which dates from the early 1700s, to become forced laborers in the Americas.

Economic development in the New World had far-reaching ramifications for both enslaved Africans and European colonizers. The commercial revolution opened up seemingly boundless markets for New World commodities like tobacco, cotton, rice, and sugar. During the 17th century, European countries and entrepreneurs scrambled to secure colonial possessions, especially in the Caribbean, to produce these profitable staples. Since European diseases and warfare had severely depleted native populations, planters experienced a severe labor shortage. A vast majority of them turned to imported African labor to clear the forests and work the plantations.

Tobacco, the first lucrative staple crop produced in the Americas, quickly glutted the market, and savvy planters began cultivating sugarcane. Sugar and its significant byproducts, molasses and rum, soon became the primary crop produced by slave labor. Slavery exploded in the Caribbean. The result was disastrous for the imported labor force: overcrowding led to severe outbreaks of communicable diseases, death rates soared, and work conditions deteriorated. But it was more profitable for planters to import newer, "fresher" laborers than to care for those already working fields in places like Cuba, Jamaica, and Barbados. With new slaves constantly arriving from Africa, Caribbean planters and overseers developed a system to "break in" newcomers. After being "broken" (in spirit as well as in the habits of freedom) slaves were sometimes re-exported to places like Mexico and North America.

Traditionally, historians have depicted the trans-Atlantic slave trade as a triangle connecting points in western Europe, West Africa, and the Americas. Slave ships first departed from European ports, sailed to Africa, brought their human cargo to the American coast, and returned home. This triangle, however, leaves out the important Caribbean "slave breaking"

Right: Engraving showing a cross section of a slave ship.

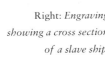

link. The slave trade really resembled a lopsided rectangle. Here is how the trade (and the slave economy) worked:

European ships (most west European countries participated in the trade) filled their holds with African slaves in "factories" like Cape Coast Castle or Elmina. In Caribbean ports they replaced most of the slaves in their holds with products like rum and molasses, and sailed for North America. In ports like Charleston and Boston, the remaining slaves and Caribbean products were traded for North American commodities like furs and fish. Traders concluded the rectangle when they unloaded their merchandise back in Lisbon or Liverpool.

The African dispersion and the "triangle trade"

→ European and American slave trade route

→ Arab and Ottoman slave trade route

Slavery in British North America, 1633–1755

African slave labor was vital to the economic life of British North America. During the 17th century slavery spread into each of the four main regions colonized by England: the Caribbean, the southern, the middle, and the New England colonies. The institution became most entrenched in colonies that exported labor-intensive commodities like sugar, rum, rice, indigo, tobacco, pitch, and turpentine. This meant that the African populations were largest in the Caribbean (where most sugar was produced), the Chesapeake colonies of Maryland and Virginia (which exported tobacco), and the Carolinas (which produced rice, indigo, and small amounts of cotton). In the middle colonies of Pennsylvania, New Jersey, and New York, slaves were used primarily as servants and laborers. New England had the fewest number of slaves in British America because the region was settled by Puritans, who tended to emigrate as families and work the land themselves. This did not, however, keep Puritans from entering and eventually dominating the intercolonial trade in slaves.

The transition to slave labor from labor performed by free people and indentured servants was a complex one, and spanned most of the 17th century. Virginia settlers had enslaved local Indians as early as 1610, but gave up the practice in the face of massive Indian raids and attacks. The switch to African, perpetual, race-based slavery was slow: there were only 1,600 Africans in North America in 1640, with almost a third of them in Dutch New York. During the next four decades slavery was explicitly legalized in Massachusetts (1641), Connecticut (1650), Virginia (1661), Maryland (1663), New York (1665), and South Carolina (1682). Even before it legally recognized slavery in 1663, Maryland lawmakers had mandated slavery as a lifelong condition for Africans and their children; Virginia classified slavery as a lifelong, inheritable, and "racial" status for blacks in 1670. The remaining colonies of British North America legalized slavery in the early 18th century.

With the growth of the institution of slavery in all the British colonies, lawmakers turned their attention to the regulation of slaves' lives. The resulting "slave codes" routinely forbade teaching slaves to read and write; outlawed group gatherings outside of church and contact with free blacks; and required slaves to carry written passes when not on plantation grounds. South Carolina's code, for example, defended the need for legal controls by citing the "barbarous, wild, savage natures [of Africans], rendering them wholly unqualified to be governed by the laws, customs, and practices of this Province." The statute continued: "all negroes, mulatoes, mustizoes or Indians . . . hereafter shall be bought and sold for slaves, are hereby declared slaves; and they, and their children, are hereby made and declared slaves, to all intents and purposes." Life servitude for Africans and their children was becoming a legal reality in British North America.

In Maryland and Virginia, the deteriorating status of black people extended to social relationships as well. Other states quickly followed their lead. In 1664, for example, Maryland passed a law stipulating that a white woman who married a slave would have to serve the slave's master as long as her husband lived.

Maryland's law, in turn, set the pattern for other colonies to penalize black-white marriages.

Not all blacks and slaves lived in the South or performed agricultural labor on rural plantations. Cities and towns on the eastern seaboard contained large African populations as early as the mid-17th century. As cosmopolitan population centers, these cities would always attract free and enslaved blacks and nurture movements and agitation for black rights. Philadelphia, originally settled by anti-slavery Quakers, had the largest free black population in North America. Black Philadelphians helped found the city's schools, literary societies, churches, and fraternal organizations. By 1741, slaves constituted one fifth of the population of New York City, and caused a panic that year when authorities heard that blacks were planning to burn the city and kill all the whites. Calling it the "Great Negro Plot," city leaders arrested 154 blacks and 24 whites, accusing them of conspiracy. Other cities were centers of African colonial life as well: in Baltimore, skilled and unskilled black artisans worked as dockworkers, blacksmiths, coopers, and domestics. Savannah and Charleston quickly became major centers for the importation of slaves from the West Indies and Africa. And the capital of Virginia, Richmond, had the largest percentage of black residents of any city in the 18th century.

MAINE
(part of Massachusetts)

NEW YORK
1665

NH
1714

Portsmouth

1641

Salem
Boston

MASSACHUSETTS

Plymouth

CONN.
1650

Newport

RI
1703

New York

New Haven

New London

PENNSYLVANIA
1700

1702

Philadelphia

NEW JERSEY

Baltimore

1721

1663–64 DELAWARE

MARYLAND

VIRGINIA
1661

St. Marys

Williamsburg

Richmond

Edenton

NORTH CAROLINA
1715

SOUTH CAROLINA
1682

GEORGIA
1755

Charleston

Port Royal

Savannah

N

| 0 | 100 km |
| 0 | 100 miles |

Major African population centers in colonial North America, 1633–1755

• major colonial port

● major center of slave population

→ African slave trading route

1714 year slavery legalized

Blacks in British North America, 1680–1740

Before 1700, black people constituted only a small minority in colonial North America. In 1680, Africans in Virginia (the state with the highest numbers of blacks) composed just 7 percent of the population. Even in South Carolina, which in the 18th century would have a black majority, Africans made up just 17 percent of the population. All this would change in the years after each colony defined the legal status of slaves. With slavery redefined as an inherited, racial status, planters purchased more and more Africans.

What was it like for these Africans? First, it must be underscored that Africans in America, unlike their European counterparts, were forced to immigrate. They were kidnapped and captured from their homes and families, forced to endure the Middle Passage, and sold into a life of toil for others. Second, they had to learn to communicate with whites and even other slaves, many of whom came from different ethnic groups and spoke different languages. Very early on, Africans developed a form of speech that was uniquely their own, combining words, grammatical structures and linguistic traditions. Overall, scholars agree that life for these first African immigrants was full of isolation and alienation.

By 1740, a major demographic shift had occurred. A black population of numerical significance could be found in several colonies, and new arrivals from Africa and the Caribbean would have likely encountered people who shared their religious beliefs, kinship arrangements, language, and (enslaved) status. Also springing into existence by the 1740s was a rapidly expanding native-born population, whose identities spanned two continents and whose experiences laid the groundwork for a new, African American culture. Thus for blacks in British America in the mid-18th century, it became possible to forge a common new culture that retained much of their Africanness. These new immigrants laid the foundations of black America.

The Stono Revolt

At the same time blacks were developing their own cultures of work, belief, family, and identity, slavery became more entrenched in American law and practice. Slaves did not accept these changes passively. On hundreds of plantations and homes in all 13 colonies, slaves learned to work slowly, break tools, steal from their masters, tell stories of resistance, and, in some cases, rebel with violence. In 1739, slaves on the Stono Plantation 20 miles outside Charleston, South Carolina, decided to risk their lives for freedom. The rebellion began when 20 slaves stole guns and ammunition from a nearby store. The armed slaves then headed south for the border with Spanish Florida, a sparsely populated and well-known haven for runaway slaves. En route, they burned and raided several plantations, killing white residents and freeing slaves, swelling their numbers to more than 80. As they reached the Savannah River the slaves were caught and

The Stono revolt, 1739–40

high slave concentration

low slave concentration

SOUTH CAROLINA

Stono Plantation's revolt

Savannah River

Charleston

Port Royal

N

0   100 km

0   100 miles

ambushed by the better-armed South Carolina militia, which massacred the runaways. In a chilling act, the militia then beheaded the slaves and lined the road with their heads as a warning to other slaves planning similar revolts.

After the Stono rebellion, one of the most successful slave revolts of the time, South Carolina and the other southern colonies passed harsher slave codes to regulate the movements of both slaves and free blacks. Especially concerned were white South Carolinians, who were out-numbered by blacks two to one. Stono also struck fear about expanding slavery into the hearts of Northern slave owners. This fear of revolt only increased as the colonies grew more and more dependent on slavery and a rising population of enslaved African Americans.

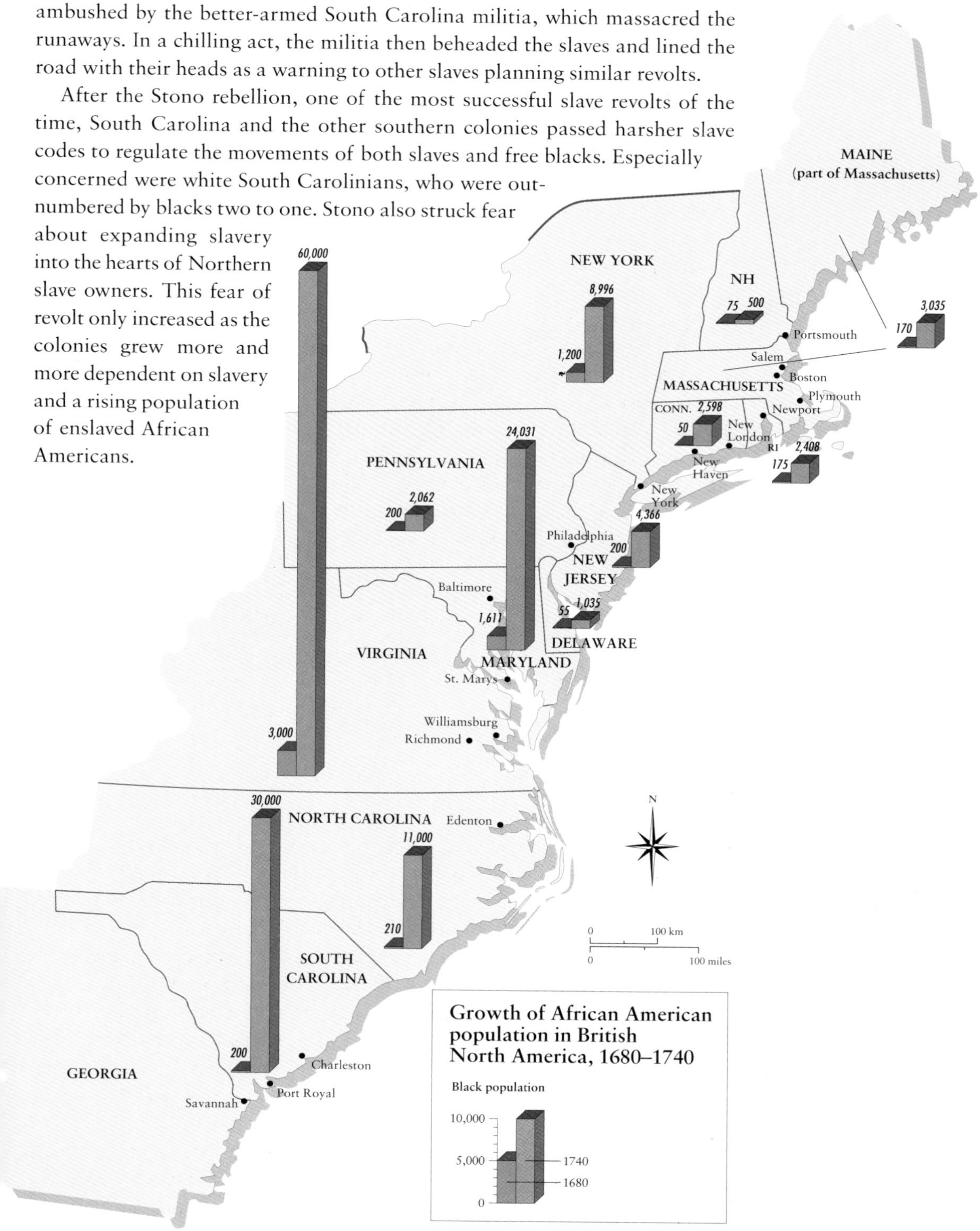

MAINE
(part of Massachusetts)

NEW YORK
60,000
8,996
1,200

NH
75 500
Portsmouth
170
3,035

Salem
Boston
MASSACHUSETTS Plymouth
CONN. 2,598 Newport
50 New London
New Haven
RI 175 2,408

PENNSYLVANIA
24,031
2,062
200
New York
4,366
Philadelphia
200
NEW JERSEY
Baltimore
1,611
55 1,035
DELAWARE
VIRGINIA MARYLAND
St. Marys
Williamsburg
Richmond
3,000

NORTH CAROLINA Edenton
30,000
11,000

N

210

SOUTH CAROLINA

0   100 km
0   100 miles

Growth of African American
population in British
North America, 1680–1740

Black population

GEORGIA
200
Charleston
Port Royal
Savannah

10,000

5,000 1740
1680

0

29

Black Population on the Eve of the Revolution

During the 18th century, two vastly different societies emerged in the American colonies—one white and free and another black and, for the most part, unfree. (Native Americans overwhelmingly lived on the borders of European and black settlement, and within their own nations.) No longer were African Americans isolated on rural plantations: by the time the United States gained its independence the black population had surpassed 500,000. In the middle of the 18th century another watershed occurred as well: for the first time since Africans arrived in North America in 1619, a Creole or locally born black population began to emerge. These Creoles drew strongly on the cultural influences of their African ancestors, but supplemented them with new, hybridized practices and traditions from America, the only home they ever knew. These were the beginnings of the vibrant African American society that exists today.

This watercolor from the 1700s depicts slaves performing a West African dance called the "juba." The banjo fashioned from a gourd and the twisted leather drumsticks are also of African origin, and illustrate the persistence of African cultural heritage in the American colonies.

For the white, free, and dominant society, the mid-18th century was a time of escalating crises with Great Britain. Many colonists questioned the right of the British Parliament to force them to comply with legislation like the Sugar and Stamp Acts, and likened themselves to slaves. It no doubt struck enslaved blacks as ironic when slaveholding patriots like George Washington, Thomas Jefferson, and Patrick Henry demanded liberty and an end to British tyranny. The fact that American independence was in many ways purchased with slave labor, and some of the most eloquent pleas for freedom came from the colonies' largest slaveholders, was labeled the "American paradox" by the historian Edmund Morgan. Yet the revolutionary philosophy that the patriots

honed—culminating in Jefferson's words that all men, being created equal, were endowed with the "unalienable Rights . . . of Life, Liberty, and the pursuit of Happiness"—had powerful implications for blacks and other oppressed minorities. But this battle over the meaning of the Declaration would not take place in the 1770s, or even later in the 18th century; the nation's founding document did not even mention slavery and the slave trade. Jefferson's first draft of the Declaration did contain a factually inaccurate (and anti-slavery) passage blaming George III for the slave trade—but it was excised by a powerful bloc of Southern slaveholders who were perfectly satisfied to make lies out of "self-evident truths."

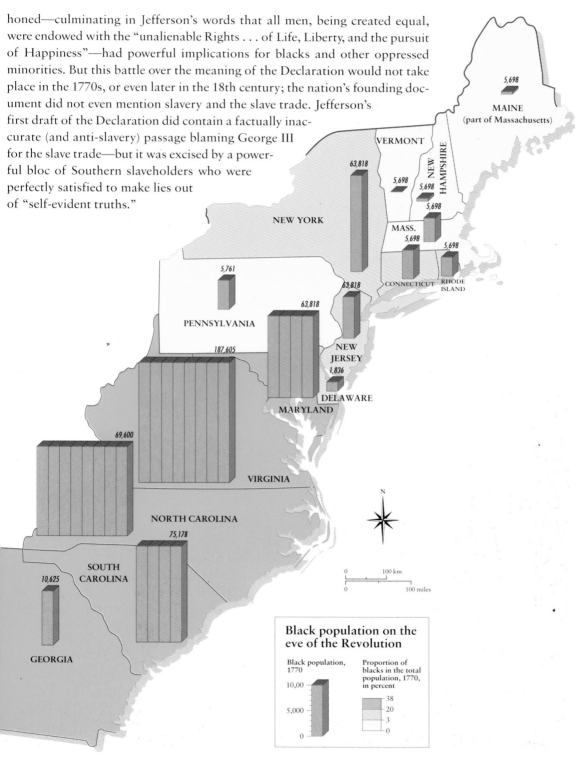

MAINE
(part of Massachusetts)

5,698

VERMONT

NEW HAMPSHIRE

63,818

5,698

5,698

5,698

NEW YORK

MASS.
5,698

5,698

5,761

63,818

CONNECTICUT   RHODE ISLAND

63,818

PENNSYLVANIA

NEW JERSEY

187,605

1,836

DELAWARE

MARYLAND

69,600

VIRGINIA

NORTH CAROLINA

75,178

SOUTH CAROLINA

10,625

GEORGIA

0   100 km

0   100 miles

N

Black population on the eve of the Revolution

Black population, 1770

10,00

5,000

0

Proportion of blacks in the total population, 1770, in percent

38
20
3
0

PART II: TWO COMMUNITIES, SLAVE AND FREE

And about this time I had a vision—and I saw white spirits and black spirits engaged in battle, and the sun was darkened—the thunder rolled in the Heavens, and blood flowed in the streams— and I heard a voice saying, "Such is your luck, such you are called to see, and let it come rough or smooth, you must surely bear it."
—Nat Turner, 1831

A British naval officer painted this watercolor depicting conditions below deck on the slave ship Albanez *in about 1840. Millions of Africans died of disease, dehydration, and suicide during the Middle Passage.*

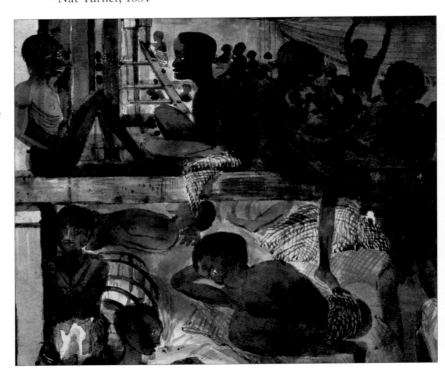

Slavery was well established in all 13 British colonies by the time a movement for independence began. What's more, slave labor had become the cornerstone of the economic system in every colony south of the Pennsylvania border. Across the South a body of laws called slave codes emerged, codifying the fact that slaves were property, not people. Laws were enacted to protect this property, and to protect whites when their property became "troublesome." That these laws were often enacted by the same men who decried British tyranny is at the center of the "American Paradox." Still the movement for independence from Great Britain was in many ways linked with the problem of slavery, and numerous African Americans attempted to make the Revolution a war for freedom, as both patriots and loyalists. The Massachusetts-born Patriot Prince Hall saw the implications of his own struggle as well as that of his nation—he fought for human freedom as well as political independence. On the other side, thousands of African American slaves saw the British army—which announced that any slave joining them in arms would be set free—not as an army of oppression, but one of liberation.

After the war was over, the surging revolutionary ideology set in motion a process that historians have termed the "First Emancipation." Within a generation of independence from Great Britain, every state in what was becoming the "North" either abolished chattel slavery or made provisions for gradual emancipation. This process dramatically increased the number of free blacks in the new nation. Free blacks always occupied a precarious place in American society, somewhere between slavery and true freedom. Although not legally property, they were perceived by most whites as inferior. Racist ideology and laws passed by whites denied free blacks their rights and legitimized their treatment as second-class citizens. For example, Congress barred free blacks from serving in the militia in 1792; 18 years later they were banned from delivering the mail. Many of the same states that enacted gradual abolition statutes after the Revolution revoked voting rights from free blacks in the early 19th century. Yet despite rampant discrimination, African Americans in the North intensified their struggle for their own inalienable rights, while also attacking the ongoing system of slavery in the South. In Northern cities, growing communities of free African Americans resisted terrible discrimination to found newspapers, open businesses, and even create their own church.

In the South, slavery was reinvigorated after the Revolution, largely due to the invention of the cotton gin, which made cotton cultivation wildly profitable. Enslaved blacks built an empire based on staple crops in the fertile bottomlands of Alabama, Mississippi, and Georgia. But slaves created more than wealth to be exploited by their white owners. When they left the fields at the end of the day, enslaved blacks tended to their families, their spirituality, and their humanity. They played instruments and danced to a hybridized, African American music. They built strong family bonds in the face of slave law and forced separations. And they fashioned an African American religion that emphasized liberation and a coming day of judgment. "The idea of a revolution in the conditions of the whites and the blacks," said the escaped slave Charles Ball, "is the cornerstone of the religion of the latter."

Slaves used more than religion and family life to resist the inhumanity of slavery. On several occasions, they hatched violent conspiracies and revolts. Denmark Vesey, a free African American from Charleston, planned the city's fiery destruction in 1822. Before the revolt could take place, however, authorities hanged Vesey and 34 other conspirators. Nine years later, the Virginia slave and lay preacher Nat Turner led some 60 slaves in a revolt that left 55 white men, women, and children dead.

During the half century following the Revolution, blacks in slavery and freedom created a culture of their own. They launched assaults on slavery and built institutions. And they prepared themselves for an even greater struggle: to force the United States to live up to the promises and pronouncements in the Declaration of Independence.

The First Emancipation

The War for Independence and the revolutionary ideals of liberty and freedom set in motion forces that forever changed the status of blacks in the North. In 1776, few revolutionaries would have predicted that their arguments against British "tyranny" would also be applied to the tyranny faced by slaves. But that is precisely what happened. Voices rose across the North to contrast the hypocrisy of a war waged for liberty from England on the one hand and the continued existence of human thralldom on the other.

Within a generation, every state in what was becoming the "North" either abolished chattel slavery or made provisions for gradual emancipation. Historians term this the "First Emancipation" (the second would come in the wake of the Civil War). But racism survived the revolutionary era: blacks in the North might have been free, but they were certainly not equal. And in the South, planters were able to stem the anti-slavery tide and build an economy even more dependent on human bondage.

Many black soldiers earned their freedom with their service in the Revolution, and in effect "freed" themselves. Others were emancipated by their state legislatures. The effect of African Americans taking up arms in the war was dramatic: nearly every state that enlisted slaves to serve in the army either freed them immediately or promised manumission at the end of their service.

Residents of the new state of Vermont outlawed slavery when they drafted a constitution in 1777. In some states, emancipation acts were the result of pressure exerted by the slaves themselves. In Massachusetts, where the state's 1780 bill of rights claimed that all people were born "free and equal," an enterprising slave named Elizabeth Freeman sued for freedom and won in 1781, making her surname a reality. Not only did the county court of Great Barrington rule in Freeman's favor—the court also awarded her damages against her former master. Two years later, the chief justice of the Supreme Judicial Court, influenced by Freeman's and other slaves' suits for freedom—declared that the court was "fully of the opinion that perpetual servitude can no longer be tolerated in our government." Hundreds of slaves promptly declared themselves free in Massachusetts and New Hampshire and left their masters.

Legislation was necessary to end slavery in the other Northern states. Pennsylvania, which had a large anti-slavery Quaker population, led the way in 1780 with the first "gradual" emancipation statute in modern history. A state law declared that no black person born after that date could be held in bondage after he or she turned 28. In 1784 Rhode Island and Connecticut followed with their own gradual emancipation statutes. Slaveholders in New York and New Jersey, which had far higher slave populations than the other Northern states, were successful in stalling similar legislation for years. Not until 1799 (New York) and 1804 (New Jersey) did these last two Northern states pass complete gradual emancipation laws. It is important to remember that these gradual emancipation statutes freed no one immediately (adults remained slaves until they were set free or died, and children performed more than two decades of uncompensated labor) and that they were rarely the product of a principled philosophical stance. More often than not Northern whites responded to a combination of conscience, pragmatism, and their own self-interest.

In 1787 Congress passed the Northwest Ordinance (written by Thomas Jefferson), which outlawed slavery and involuntary servitude in the territories north and west of the Ohio River, thus marking out the future states of Ohio, Michigan, Indiana, Illinois, and Wisconsin as free states. The First Emancipation seemed to be gaining steam in the Upper South as well: Virginia, Maryland, and North Carolina passed legislation after the Revolution making it easier for owners to manumit their slaves. But that was as far as the postwar anti-slavery movement got. In fact, in a reaction against the change sweeping the nation after independence, Southern slaveholders and conservatives joined ranks to insert protections for the institution in the new federal Constitution. Emancipation in the South, they argued, would ruin the planter class and amount to a radical and dangerous social revolution. The First Emancipation was stopped in its tracks.

VERMONT
1777

1780

NH
1783

M A S S A C H U S E T T S
1780

1799
NEW YORK

CONN.
1784

RI
1784

PENNSYLVANIA
1780

1804
NEW
JERSEY

NORTHWEST
TERRITORY
1787

MARYLAND
DELAWARE

KENTUCKY
TERRITORY

VIRGINIA

TENNESSEE
TERRITORY

NORTH CAROLINA

MISSISSIPPI
TERRITORY

SOUTH
CAROLINA

GEORGIA

0   100 km

0   100 miles

N

The First Emancipation

1783 date of emancipation

slavery prohibited by Northwest Ordinance 1787

slavery banned by state constitution

gradual emancipation by statute

slavery allowed by law

35

Free Blacks in the New Republic

By the beginning of the 19th century there were rapidly growing communities of free blacks in most Northern states. A large majority of free blacks flocked to cities. Philadelphia and New York had long had sizable free black populations, and after the First Emancipation these communities grew dramatically. Free African Americans fled the declining economic opportunities in the countryside in search of a better life in the city.

Urban free black communities were also havens for runaway slaves from the Upper South, where the grip of slavery was growing firmer. In 1800, both New York City's and Philadelphia's populations were more than 10 percent black.

A small minority of the blacks in seaport cities became wealthy entrepreneurs, like the Massachusetts ship builder Paul Cuffe. Others became skilled artisans. Most, however, settled into stable but low-paying jobs as waiters, porters, barbers, coachmen, street vendors, and maids. Numerous sailors, dockworkers, and day laborers at the turn of the century were free blacks.

Free blacks constantly had to struggle with fears of re-enslavement (it was not uncommon for free blacks to be kidnapped and sold into slavery) and the realities of living in a larger society that often despised them. African Americans responded by building strong institutions of their own: black churches, Masonic lodges, schools, and relief societies were created at a dizzying rate around 1800. These institutions joined black dance halls, gambling houses, and saloons as the only racially integrated establishments in Northern cities.

Numerous free blacks made outstanding contributions during the period following the First Emancipation.

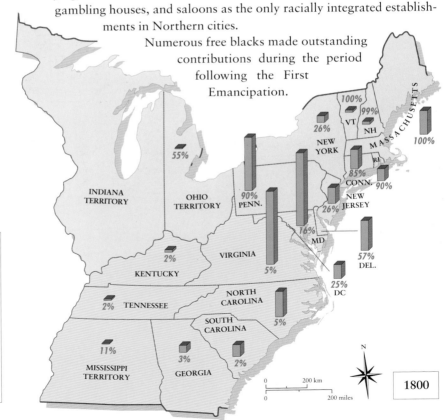

Free black population

- free state
- slave state

10
5
0
free black population, in thousands

50% proportion of free blacks in the total black population

1800

Ex-slave Phillis Wheatley became internationally renowned for her poetry; Benjamin Banneker made important advances in astronomy and surveying; and the gifted author Olaudah Equiano helped found the modern anti-slavery movement with his volume *The Interesting Narrative of the Life of Olaudah Equino, or Gustavus Vassa, the African.*

Much had happened to change these free black communities by 1830. First, the gradual manumission laws passed during the First Emancipation worked: there were only a handful of aging blacks who remained enslaved in the North. Second, with the exception of the Upper South, almost all Southern blacks were slaves. And the slave population had shifted dramatically after 1800, from the Atlantic seaboard states of Maryland, Virginia, the Carolinas, and Georgia to the Gulf states of Florida, Alabama, Mississippi, Louisiana, and Texas.

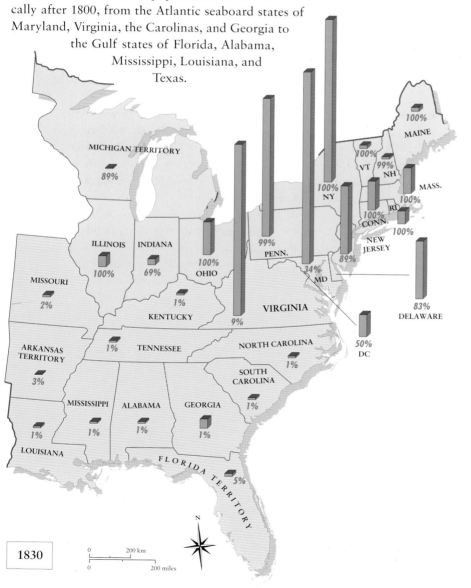

1830

Discrimination in the Antebellum North

Official and unofficial discrimination against free African Americans increased in the early 19th century. At the same time that white men experienced a significant expansion of their rights, especially in terms of voting, free blacks saw their rights eroding in both the North and the South. Many of these erosions were for rights guaranteed in the U.S. Constitution: by 1835, for example, the right of free assembly had been revoked for nearly all of the South's free blacks. They were barred by law from carrying firearms without a license in Virginia, Maryland, and North Carolina. And African Americans in the South were forbidden to hold religious services without the presence of a licensed and "respectable" white minister. Things were little better in the North. Several states followed Pennsylvania's lead in requiring free blacks to work and mandating that their means of support be visible. At the same time, African Americans were almost completely eliminated from the better-paying skilled trades as well as work on the docks, in warehouses, or in the merchant marine. One African American newspaper complained that blacks "have ceased to be hackney coachmen and draymen, and they are now almost displaced as stevedores. They are rapidly losing their places as barbers and servants. Ten families employ white servants now, where one did 20 years ago." A large array of the most menial jobs acquired the contemptuous epithet "nigger work," labor that African Americans performed because it was the only paying work they could get.

Nowhere was discrimination more pronounced in the early republic than in matters of suffrage. For white men, the early 19th century (the "era of the common man") represented a time of expanded suffrage and rights. Free blacks, on the other hand, were routinely barred from the polls. In a bill signed by Thomas Jefferson in 1802, they were excluded from the polls in the newly designated capital of Washington, D.C. Free blacks who had voted for years in Maryland, Tennessee, North Carolina, and Pennsylvania were barred from doing so in 1810, 1834, 1835, and 1838, respectively. New York erected a property qualification of $250 for black voters at the same time it eliminated all such requirements for whites. Between 1819 and 1865, every new state restricted the suffrage to whites. By 1840, the high-water mark for participation by registered (i.e., white male) voters, 93 percent of the free black population of the United States was disfranchised. "An educated colored man in the United States," wrote the abolitionist Frederick Douglass, "unless he has within him the heart of a hero, and is willing to engage in a life-long battle for his rights, as a man, finds few inducements to remain in this country. He is isolated in the land of his birth—debarred by his color from congenial association with whites; he is equally cast out by the ignorance of blacks." Douglass didn't have to mention the even higher barriers erected against black women and uneducated black men.

MISSOU

ARKANS

LOUISIA

MICHIGAN TERRITORY

MAINE

VERMONT

NH

NEW YORK

MASSACHUSETTS

CONN.   RI

LLINOIS

INDIANA

OHIO

PENNSYLVANIA

NEW JERSEY

MARYLAND

Washington, DC

DELAWARE

KENTUCKY

VIRGINIA

TENNESSEE

NORTH CAROLINA

SOUTH CAROLINA

SSISSIPPI

ALABAMA

GEORGIA

FLORIDA

N

0   200 km

0   200 miles

Free black disfranchisement, 1840

Free blacks barred from voting

black suffrage with restrictions

no restrictions

The Free Black Community

The AME Church

African Americans responded to discrimination by creating institutions of their own. The most enduring of these institutions was the African Methodist Episcopal Church, founded in 1790 by the Rev. Richard Allen. Allen saved enough money to purchase his freedom from his Delaware owner in 1777, the same year he experienced a powerful religious conversion. In 1786 he moved to Philadelphia, home to a thriving free black population, and became an itinerant preacher. At first Allen opposed a separate church for blacks, but eventually came to believe that African Americans needed their own organizations to guarantee their autonomy and make their voices heard. Allen, Absalom Jones, and James Forten first established a secular mutual aid society called the Free African Society. Then, in 1794, Allen organized and dedicated the Bethel Church, later known as the Bethel African Methodist Episcopal Church.

Branches of the new AME church quickly appeared in Baltimore, Wilmington, and smaller towns in Pennsylvania and New Jersey. In 1816, the various congregations were officially bound together in a formal organization. Theologically, the members of the church were Methodists, and their numbers grew rapidly. By 1820 there were 4,000 black Methodists in Philadelphia, and nearly half that many in Baltimore. The church even made inroads as far west as Pittsburgh and as far south as Charleston, before the Denmark Vesey slave conspiracy halted the growth of black organizations there. By 1826 the AME Church had almost 8,000 members, and grew to more than 50,000 in 1860 and 500,000 in 1892. The denomination continues to grow today, encompassing more than 3,600 churches worldwide.

Growth of the African Methodist Episcopal Church (AME), 1816–92

1816–26 | 1827–56 | 1857–92

African American Newspapers

Free blacks organized far more than religious denominations. Black Masonic lodges attracted hundreds of members, as did black schools, social clubs, lodges, and mutual aid societies. Black restaurants, dance halls, and saloons also dotted free black communities, and were often the only places where blacks and whites met socially. Free African Americans also published scores of newspapers and periodicals to resist discrimination and stake their claim to civil equality. New Yorkers John Russwurm and Samuel Cornish published the first edition of *Freedom's Journal*, the earliest sustained black newspaper, in 1827 (a paper called the *African Intelligencer* had existed briefly in Washington, D.C., in 1820). Committed to civil rights for African Americans, the paper folded after Russwurm emigrated to Liberia. Like many of the paper's successors, it was short-lived, mostly because of financial pressures and a small (often illiterate) readership.

Ten years later Cornish commenced publication of the *Colored American*, which weighed in strongly on the issue of a suitable name for the emerging African American community. "Let us and our friends unite, in baptizing the term 'Colored Americans,' and henceforth let us be written of, preached of, and prayed for as such. It is the true term, and one which is above reproach." Other papers like the *National Watchman*, the *Weekly Anglo-African* and the *Mirror of Liberty* joined in the debate, and gave expression to a growing community. The most successful black journalist of the antebellum period also joined the debate, but Frederick Douglass, editor of the *North Star*, preferred the term "American." Like other editors, Douglass suffered from financial problems and threats of violence, but his paper and its successor endured for more than a decade.

African American newspapers and periodicals, 1820–60

- city with 5 or more African American newspapers and/or periodicals
- city with fewer than 5 African American newspapers and/or periodicals

The Cotton Kingdom

The Antebellum Slave Economy

In 1793 a technological innovation revolutionized Southern agriculture and substantially altered the lives of many African Americans. Great Britain's newly minted textile barons were willing to pay dearly for cotton, but American planters couldn't bear the labor costs required to prepare the crop for export. The problem wasn't the climate (short-staple cotton thrived in the warm, humid climate of the Deep South) or the labor—it was the cotton plant's sticky seeds. Before cotton could be milled, the seeds needed to be removed by hand, a daylong task for a slave cleaning just 1 pound of cotton. By fashioning a machine (or "gin") that combed the seeds from cotton fiber with metal pins on rollers, the Yankee inventor Eli Whitney rejuvenated plantation agriculture in the South. Now a single worker (usually an enslaved African American) could clean 50 pounds of cotton a day.

As a direct result of the cotton gin, slavery spread rapidly south and west. Chesapeake planters, whose land was north of the cotton line, sold their slaves to Alabama, Georgia, and Mississippi, often for huge profits. The movement of

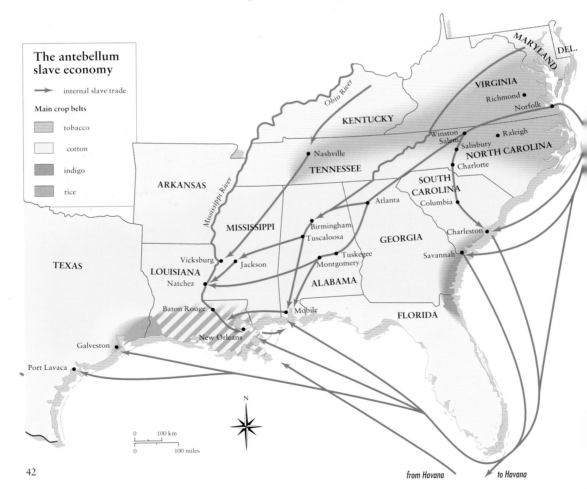

slaves out of the Chesapeake was fast and furious: in 1790, planters in Maryland and Virginia owned 56 percent of all American slaves; by 1860 they owned just 15 percent.

In the years between the invention of the cotton gin and the closing of the slave trade in 1808, more than 250,000 slaves were brought directly to the United States. Seeking profits from the booming demand for cotton, white and black Southerners pushed southeastern Indians and Mexicans in Texas out of their way. In 1850, fully three quarters of all slaves were agricultural laborers: fifty-five percent grew cotton; 10 percent grew rice, hemp, and sugar; and 10 percent grew tobacco. For slaves who were not agricultural laborers, leading occupations were turpentine producer, lumberjack, miner, dock worker, textile worker, and industrial laborer.

Significant Plantations of the Antebellum South

The explosion of slavery into the South and West changed the way enslaved African Americans worked and lived. In the Chesapeake, where agriculture shifted from tobacco production to grain and livestock, more slaves were trained as skilled artisans.

Significant plantations in the antebellum South

- plantation
- skilled labor, mixed agriculture
- lowland task labor
- gang labor

Their work, though complex, required little supervision. Skilled slaves, who were almost always men, were often hired out to work for wages in towns and cities. Women mostly worked under close supervision weeding, hoeing, and maintaining the fields. The large plantations of the 18th century, like Thomas Jefferson's Monticello, largely converted to mixed agriculture by 1800.

In the lowland coastal regions of Georgia and South Carolina, where deadly diseases threatened the lives of both slaves and slave owners, the "task system" prevailed. Slaves were given a daily "task" and allowed to complete it at his or her own pace. This encouraged hard work and took little supervision—and slaves often turned the task system to their own advantage. On many of the region's immense plantations, which included Rose Hill, Ocean Plantation, and Hampton, slaves won the right to cultivate their own "private fields" and sell their products on the open market. The owners of these busy slaves were among the richest Americans, and were therefore tolerant of the slaves' own commercial activity.

In the new cotton lands of the Deep South, however, slaves had very little independence. Cotton cultivation demanded intensive and skilled labor. Slaves on cotton plantations routinely worked in "gangs" from sunup until sundown, under the watchful eye (and whips) of white overseers. Plantations like The Hermitage (owned by President Andrew Jackson) and Melrose in Mississippi reaped tremendous profits from the labor of hundreds of slaves.

This 1862 photograph depicts five generations of a slave family on a South Carolina plantation, illustrating a highly complex network of kin relationships. Despite the horrors of separation and sale, the black family survived slavery.

Slave
population
distribution

. 2,000 slaves

1830

1860

0   200 km

0   200 miles

N

The Slave Community

Slave Life: Hopeton Plantation, Georgia

According to the 1850 U.S. Census, 1.8 million slaves, or more than half the slaves in the United States, worked on cotton farms or plantations. Thus the cotton plantation was the typical locale for the enslaved African American. On smaller farms, slaves and their owners often worked together in the fields. But the larger plantations were among the most intensely commercialized and specialized farms in the world. Factorylike organization and division of labor was the rule.

The slaves' labor—the exploitation of which provided the economic foundation for the Old South—was the primary concern of the slave owner. The labor force was divided into two distinct groups: house slaves and field hands. Typically under the watchful eye of the slave mistress, house servants cared for children, prepared meals, cleaned the house, yards, and gardens. The field hands were a much larger group. Cotton requires a long growing season and constant attention: slaves worked planting, hoeing, weeding, picking, and preparing the cotton crop for market. Field hands also tended livestock and the large corn and other vegetable fields that fed all the residents of the plantation. Clearing land, burning brush, and maintaining fences and buildings were also the duties of field hands.

Labor on a cotton plantation was almost always performed under the supervision of the owner or overseer. Gangs of slaves were told when to work, when to rest, and when to quit. There was little incentive for the slaves to work hard or develop initiative under this system; in fact, slaves usually worked as slowly as they could without incurring punishment. Whippings were common in an attempt to extract more work from field slaves. Planters justified this practice with racism: African Americans, they reasoned, were a childlike race and required strict punishment.

William Henry Brown created this collage depicting a slave harvest crew near Vicksburg, Mississippi, in 1842. Note that during the busy cotton harvest, even children helped in the fields.

Hopeton Plantation in Glynn County, Georgia, (see map on page 43) provides an example of the complex microcosm of the plantation. Between 350 and 400 slaves performed various types of labor at Hopeton, from tending the vast rice, cotton, sugarcane, and vegetable fields to manufacturing sugar and

serving the planter's family. More than 40 slave cabins and outbuildings stood behind the "big house" occupied by the plantation's manager and part-owner James H. Couper. Slaves worked according to a modified task system under several overseers. According to one observer, both slaves and overseers were punished if work quotas were not met: "as the task of each [slave] is separate, imperfect work can readily be traced to the neglectful worker."

Despite the astonishing variety of crops and products produced at Hopeton (in this respect the plantation was unusual), it was hardly self-sufficient. Necessities such as blankets, cloth, corn, mackerel, needles, pork, salt, shoes, soap, thread, and other items were purchased throughout the year. In 1833 alone Couper had to purchase 3,800 bushels of corn, 29 barrels of prime pork, 53 barrels of mackerel, and 2,710 pounds of beef to feed his African American workforce. As happened on most plantations, slaves received a weekly ration of food. Typically, an adult's share was 3 to 4 pounds of salt pork or bacon, a peck of cornmeal, some sweet potatoes and molasses. Slaves' diet did not vary: this monotonous, though more or less nutritious, regimen prevailed "day to day and week to week." Slaves were also annually issued shoes and clothes, often cheap and shoddy pieces manufactured out of slave-tended cotton in New England.

Hopeton
Plantation,
Georgia

- owner's residence
- slave quarters
- service buildings
- woods
- pasture
- idle land

Crops
- cotton
- rice
- corn
- cane
- potatoes
- peas
- barley
- pumpkins

Slave Quarters, Calvitt Plantation, Texas

Plantation living conditions were generally crowded and uncomfortable. Most plantation slaves lived in tiny, rude huts behind the slave owner's "big house." Windows and floors were very rare, as was furniture. Most slaves slept on blankets resting atop corn husks or straw. Rampant overcrowding in the quarters (far more than poor diet or overwork) was the leading threat to slaves' health. Diseases like tuberculosis and dysentery spread rapidly.

This slave cabin on the Calvitt Plantation in Robertson County, Texas, was slightly more comfortable than average. The floorplan is a square of 19 feet, with a dirt floor, fireplace for heat and cooking, and a tiny loft. A front porch provided additional living space. The cabin probably housed an extended slave family, more than eight people in all. It was in the slave quarters, away from the white masters and overseers, that African Americans constructed a community based on family, religion, music, dance, and story telling. From sunup to sundown a slave's time belonged to the master; the rest of the time, however, was his or her own. Most slaves were Christians by the early 19th century, and Christian worship was a vital part of slave culture. Not surprisingly, slave sermons de-emphasized the religion preached by slave owners (obey thy master, work hard, respect property) in favor of an expressive Christianity based on the themes of suffering and redemption. Slaves generally met in secret, often in the woods, to sing spirituals, shout, pray, and dance, away from the watchful eyes of white people.

Family was also central to life in the slave quarters, despite the painful plantation realities of family separation and sexual assault. Enslaved people depended on a wide network of kin relationships to provide emotional support and strength in addition to the everyday tasks of child rearing, food preparation, and care of the

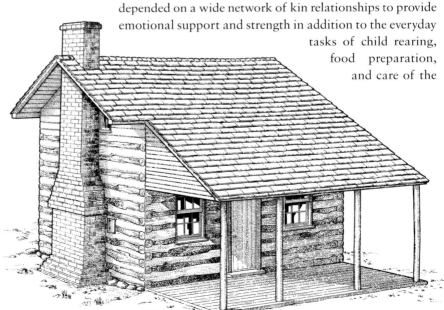

Slave quarters on Calvitt Plantation.

sick or elderly. Owners often encouraged slave marriages because they made life on the plantation more productive and peaceful; yet these families were never sanctioned by law and were always vulnerable. Because a father might live on a neighboring plantation or a mother might be sold away, large, extended kinship groups filled the slave quarters. Numerous adult relatives provided guidance, love, and protection for the children, who often treated aunts, uncles, or grandparents as if they were parents. In the face of great odds, the black family survived slavery.

That is not to say that individual families weren't destroyed by the institution: the historian Herbert Gutman has found that 29 percent of all slave marriages were broken up between 1820 and 1860. Even more families—as many as 2 million by one estimate—experienced the sale of one or more children. The ex-slave Harriet Jacobs recalled a haunting memory of seeing a mother leaving an auction house after each of her seven children had been sold: "I met that mother in the street, and her wild, haggard face lives to-day in my mind. She wrung her hands in anguish, and exclaimed, 'Gone! All gone! Why don't God kill me?'" Despite the constant threat of separation, slave families continued to have children: the right to make and maintain families was one of the most precious and well-guarded privileges slaves had.

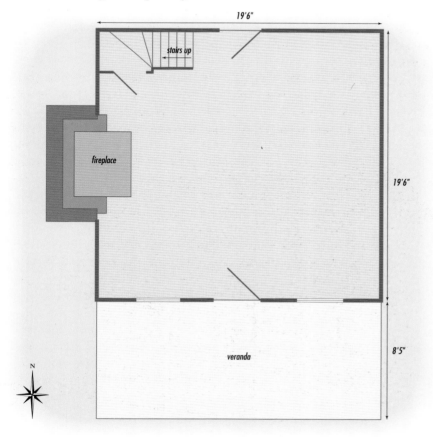

Slave quarters, Calvitt Plantation, Robertson County, Texas

Nat Turner's Rebellion, 1831

Slaves did not endure their servitude passively. They resisted in numerous ways, ranging from the barely noticeable insubordination to episodes of extreme violence. Perhaps the most common way slaves protested the continuous forced labor of plantation life was sabotage: slave hands broke tools, stole food, abused farm animals, and burned down buildings. Other day-to-day acts of resistance included slowing the pace of work, feigning illness, or self-mutilation. Slaves also used their culture to protest their situation. Songs, folk tales, and religion all helped slaves find release from hardship and suffering.

Some slaves ran away, depriving their owners of their labor. Communities of runaway slaves called Maroons existed across remote and swampy areas of the South, especially in Florida. Others, like Frederick Douglass, fought back physically against their owners and overseers.

Rebellion was, of course, the ultimate form of resistance against slavery. Most slaves understood that armed revolt was virtually suicidal. Unlike in the Caribbean, where massive slave revolts took place in Cuba, Jamaica, and most famously, Haiti, rebellion in the American South was difficult to carry out. The white population was large and maintained a near monopoly on firearms; plantations were small and relatively far apart; and panicked slaveholders responded with terror to every rumor of revolt. Still, conspiracies for escape and murder did occur. The Gabriel Prosser conspiracy rocked Richmond in 1800, and in 1822 an ex-slave named Denmark Vesey conspired to seize Charleston's armory, murder the city's white population, and escape by ship to Haiti or Africa. Slaves betrayed the plot at the last minute, and whites responded by hanging Vesey and 35 others after closed-door show trials. Southern whites' escalating fear of slave rebellion was evident by the severity and intensity with which they handled both conspiracies.

In 1829, a free African American named David Walker appealed to Southern slaves to rise up in violent rebellion: "had you not rather be killed than to be a slave to a tyrant, who takes the life of your mother, wife, and dear little children?" Black sailors sewed Walker's tract into their uniforms and spread it across the seaboard South. The next year a Virginia slave and Baptist lay preacher named Nat Turner began experiencing visions of white and black spirits engaged in battle. The son of an African woman and a father who successfully escaped to freedom, Turner learned to read and avidly studied the Bible. Believing himself an instrument of God's wrath, Turner began recruiting other slaves for a massive assault on slavery in the Tidewater.

On August 21, 1831, Turner led a small band of slaves into the home of his master, Joseph Travis, and murdered the entire family. Then, armed with pick-axes, Turner vowed to "carry terror and devastation" throughout the countryside. After attacking whites on neighboring plantations, the growing band hacked Margaret Whitehead to death with swords. The killing spree continued all night and the following day, with at least 60 slaves joining Turner's revolt. On August 23, after killing 55 white men, women, and children, the slaves were pinned down at James Parker's plantation by a group of heavily armed whites.

The next morning U.S. soldiers arrived to put down the rebellion, and most of the slaves were killed or captured. Turner escaped and eluded capture for more than two months, hiding in swamps, caves, and nearby woods.

By the time Virginia authorities apprehended, tried, and hanged Turner, whites had engaged in a retaliatory killing spree of their own. Twenty of Turner's co-conspirators were hanged, and Virginia banished ten slaves from the state. But as many as 120 African Americans, including many innocent victims, lost their lives as a result of the revolt, the bloodiest in U.S. history.

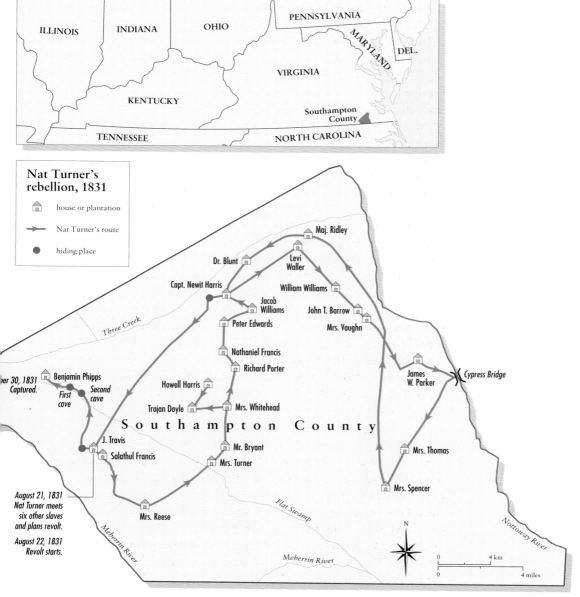

Nat Turner's rebellion, 1831

🏠 house or plantation

➤ Nat Turner's route

● hiding place

PART III: TOWARD FREEDOM

We are NATIVES of this country, we ask only to be treated as well as FOREIGNERS. Not a few of our fathers suffered and bled to purchase its independence; we ask only to be treated as well as those who fought against it. We have toiled to cultivate it . . . we ask only to enjoy the fruits of our labor. Let these moderate requests be granted, and we need not go to Africa nor anywhere else to be improved and happy.
—The Rev. Peter Williams, 1822

Slaves resisted their servitude with sabotage, by running away, and, in extraordinary cases, by inciting rebellion. But the assault on slavery was not waged by slaves alone: beginning in the 17th century, small groups of free blacks and Quakers began to attack the institution as unjust and against the will of God. By the middle of the 19th century, black and white abolitionists had fashioned the greatest reform movement of the age. Through constant agitation, they kept the slavery issue before the nation, inserting it squarely into the politics of geographic expansion. And though politicians tried again and again to compromise over the issue of slavery (in 1819, 1850, 1854, and 1857), the actions of abolitionists, slaveholders, and slaves only exacerbated the crisis between the free labor North and the slave South. Only through the catastrophe of Civil War was the destruction of slavery finally accomplished in the United States.

Opponents of slavery often disagreed on tactics and goals. Some abolitionists favored immediate emancipation and the creation of a just, anti-racist society, while most white abolitionists fell short of a belief in racial equality. Many believed that only by returning ex-slaves to Africa could the United States be rid of racial problems after emancipation. The anti-slavery movement changed dramatically between 1829 and 1831 with the publication of an influential pamphlet by David Walker and a revolutionary newspaper by William Lloyd Garrison. David Walker's *An Appeal in Four Articles* drips with angry defiance and repeatedly calls for a violent overthrow of slavery. Walker claimed that because of slavery, African Americans were the "most wretched, degraded and abject set of beings that ever lived." And unlike their white oppressors, Walker said, blacks had the capacity to forgive:

Treat us like men, and . . . we will love and respect [whites], and protect our country. . . . Treat us like men, and there is no danger but we will all live in peace and happiness together. For we are not like you . . . unforgiving. Treat us like men, and we will be your friends.

Walker, a free black Boston merchant, sewed his *Appeal* into the seams of the used clothing he sold to sailors. It was read up and down the Atlantic seaboard and helped African Americans unite in a movement for the immediate abolition of slavery.

William Lloyd Garrison, a white reformer from Massachusetts, thundered in his newspaper, the *Liberator*, that slavery was a national sin and demanded immediate emancipation. "I am in earnest," he said in his paper's inaugural issue. "I will not equivocate—I will not excuse—I will not retreat a single inch—and I will be heard!" The paper immediately won strong support from African Americans, whose patronage sustained it in its early years. In time the *Liberator* became the quasi-official organ of the American Anti-Slavery Society, founded in 1833 to abolish slavery and improve "the character and condition of the people of color."

Emboldened by the arguments of abolitionists like Walker and Garrison, black and white abolitionists greatly expanded their movement. Abolitionist societies flooded the mail with tracts and petitions. Ex-slaves like Sojourner Truth and Frederick Douglass published their narratives and went on speaking tours. Networks of sympathetic blacks and whites worked with "conductors" like Harriet Tubman to spirit runaway slaves northward on an "underground railroad." And abolitionist journals documented the daily horrors of slavery, the kidnappings of free blacks, and the tragic return of fugitives like Anthony Burns to lives of thralldom.

Born a slave in New York, Isabella Baumfree took the name Sojourner Truth in 1843 and became a prominent itinerant preacher, abolitionist, and feminist. In a famous speech in 1851, Truth attacked both racism and sexism by asking "Ain't I a woman?"

The political crisis came to a head in 1860, with the election of the anti-slavery Republican Abraham Lincoln to the presidency. Lincoln was elected on a platform of halting slavery's expansion without a single electoral vote from the South; Southern states seceded from the Union in response. The ensuing Civil War began as an effort by the North to "restore the Union." But when thousands of runaway slaves escaped behind Union lines, effectively "freeing" themselves, some Northerners began to view the war as a fight for freedom. Military necessity convinced others (including Lincoln) that the only way to win the war was to strike directly at Southern institutions like slavery. Similar sentiments led to the formation of black regiments like the 54th Massachusetts, which suffered heavy casualties fighting to destroy slavery. After the Civil War the nation commenced a bold (and, ultimately, failed) experiment to "reconstruct" the South on the basis of free labor and legal equality for African Americans. Under the protection of the Union Army, African Americans in the South were granted full civil rights, and black men were enfranchised. Several held state and national offices. But when Union troops withdrew in 1877, organizations like the Ku Klux Klan terrorized black voters and enforced racist mores extralegally. Most blacks stayed in the South and attempted to earn a living by sharecropping or tenant farming; others, however, sought a better life elsewhere and began a century of black migration to the North and West.

The Expansion of Slavery, 1819–57

The Missouri Compromise, 1820

Westward migration in the early 19th century inevitably led to tension between residents of slave and free states. Some Northerners resented the stranglehold Virginians seemed to have on the White House and the "three-fifths clause" of the U.S. Constitution, which gave slave states congressional representation based on the white population plus three fifths of the slave population. Both sections eyed each other suspiciously whenever a new state applied for entry into the Union, and were careful to maintain a balance of new slave and free states. The Northwest Ordinance of 1787 barred slavery from the territory that became the states of Ohio, Indiana, Illinois, Michigan, and Wisconsin; and the admission of Kentucky, Tennessee, Alabama, Mississippi, and Louisiana kept the number of free and slave states in balance.

When Missouri applied for admission to the Union as a state in 1819, slavery was already a way of life there. Even before the U.S. purchased Louisiana (including the parts that became Missouri), Spanish and French settlers had owned slaves. By the time the population of Missouri reached the 60,000 people required to apply for statehood, 16 percent of those people were enslaved African Americans. Missouri's application for statehood precipitated an ominous sectional crisis that threatened the unity of the nation.

Missouri Compromise, 1820

- Louisiana Purchase, 1803
- Missouri Compromise Line
- ★ state entering the Union as part of Missouri Compromise
- free state / territory, 1820
- slave state / territory, 1820

When Congress received the application, a New York representative added two amendments: one prohibiting the "further introduction of slavery" and another providing for the gradual emancipation of Missouri's 10,000 slaves. Southerners were outraged, and Congress adjourned without approving statehood. The next Congress eked out an uneasy deal known as the Missouri Compromise: Missouri would enter the Union as a slave state while the northernmost counties of Massachusetts became the free state of Maine. This scheme neutralized fears that the South would gain more influence in the U.S. Senate. Next, the South agreed to outlaw slavery north of 36°30' latitude, a line extending west from Missouri's southern border. The compromise opened up the new territory of Arkansas (present-day Oklahoma and Arkansas) to slavery while barring the institution from the remainder of the Louisiana Purchase—territory that would become the states of Kansas, Nebraska, Colorado, Minnesota, Iowa, Montana, Wyoming, and North and South Dakota.

The Missouri Compromise made plain that sectional issues were a political tinderbox. It brought the South's commitment to slavery and the North's resentment of Southern political power into direct confrontation. Thomas Jefferson, in retirement at Monticello, was distraught by the Missouri Compromise: "a geographical line, coinciding with a marked principle, moral and political, once conceived and held up to the angry passions of men, will never be obliterated," he wrote. The dispute over Missouri, "like a fire-bell in the night, awakened and filled me with terror. I considered it at once the knell of the Union."

Compromise of 1850

Thirty years after the Missouri Compromise, the issue of slavery's expansion in the West was as contentious as ever. As a result of the victory in the Mexican-American War, the United States acquired the entire Southwest: territory that would become the states of California, Nevada, Utah, New Mexico, and Arizona. Abolitionists like Frederick Douglass had done much to influence public opinion, and many anti-slavery Northerners wanted to bar slavery from spreading into territory won from Mexico. The political crisis over whether the North or the South would control the settlement of the former Mexican lands almost tore the nation apart in 1850.

Brokered by the aging Senator Henry Clay and newcomer Stephen Douglas, the Compromise of 1850 tried to appease both North and South. First, gold-rich California would be admitted as a free state, while the rest of the Mexican session would be organized without restrictions against slavery. Another provision outlawed the slave trade in the District of Columbia, where African Americans were dragged in chains and families sold apart within shouting distance of the U.S. Capitol. But to appease Southerners, Clay proposed that slavery not be abolished there. Finally, the compromise called for a new, stronger

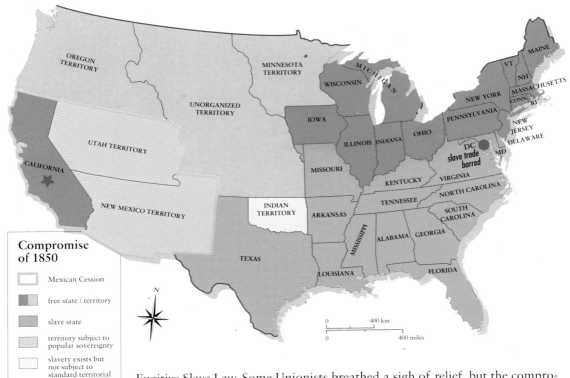

Compromise of 1850

- ☐ Mexican Cession
- ■ free state / territory
- ■ slave state
- ▨ territory subject to popular sovereignty
- ▨ slavery exists but not subject to standard territorial sovereignty
- ★ state entering the Union as part of the Compromise
- ● slave trade barred in nation's capital

Fugitive Slave Law. Some Unionists breathed a sigh of relief, but the compromise failed to fully address the chasm over slavery separating North and South.

Kansas-Nebraska Act, 1854

Just four years after the Compromise of 1850, the battle over slavery's expansion erupted again—this time in the Louisiana Purchase, where the slavery question had supposedly been settled by the Missouri Compromise line at 36°30'. With thousands of settlers retracing Meriwether Lewis and William Clark's path up the Missouri River and entrepreneurs calling for a railroad to connect San Francisco to the east, many Americans favored organizing a territory north of Indian Territory, present-day Oklahoma. Responding quickly, Congress passed a bill in 1853 creating Nebraska Territory, encompassing the area north of Indian Territory all the way to the Canadian border. Southern senators still smarting from the admission of free California in 1850 correctly foresaw that under the Missouri Compromise slavery would be prohibited in each state carved from Nebraska Territory; they desperately wanted to avoid the addition of new free states, which would further dilute their power in Congress.

Senator Stephen Douglas proposed repealing the part of the Missouri Compromise that prohibited slavery north of 36°30', arguing that "popular sovereignty," or the will of the settlers, should determine whether a state was

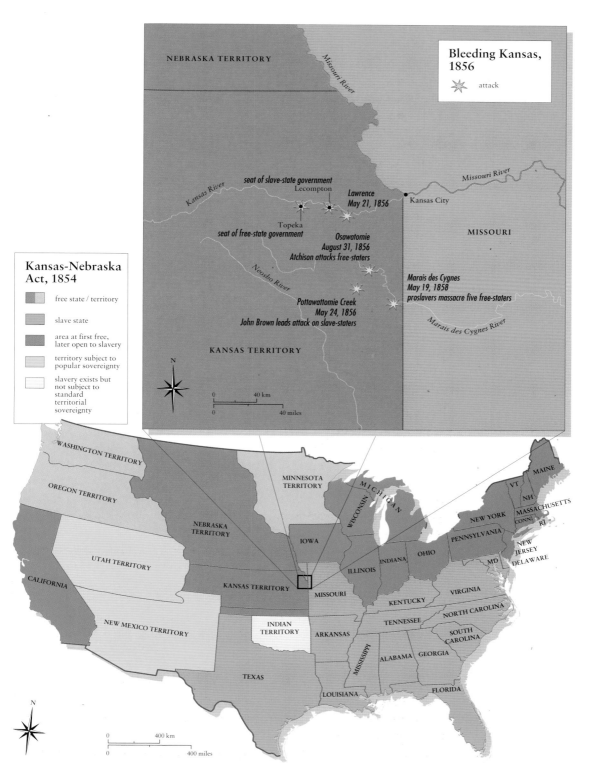

Bleeding Kansas, 1856

✳ attack

NEBRASKA TERRITORY

Missouri River

seat of slave-state government
Lecompton

Lawrence
May 21, 1856

Kansas City

Missouri River

MISSOURI

Kansas River

Topeka
seat of free-state government

Osawatomie
August 31, 1856
Atchison attacks free-staters

Neosho River

Marais des Cygnes
May 19, 1858
proslavers massacre five free-staters

Pottawattomie Creek
May 24, 1856
John Brown leads attack on slave-staters

Marais des Cygnes River

KANSAS TERRITORY

N

0   40 km
0   40 miles

Kansas-Nebraska Act, 1854

free state / territory

slave state

area at first free, later open to slavery

territory subject to popular sovereignty

slavery exists but not subject to standard territorial sovereignty

WASHINGTON TERRITORY

OREGON TERRITORY

MINNESOTA TERRITORY

MICHIGAN

WISCONSIN

MAINE

VT

NH

NEW YORK

MASSACHUSETTS

CONN RI

NEBRASKA TERRITORY

IOWA

PENNSYLVANIA

NEW JERSEY

UTAH TERRITORY

ILLINOIS

INDIANA

OHIO

MD

DELAWARE

CALIFORNIA

KANSAS TERRITORY

MISSOURI

VIRGINIA

KENTUCKY

NEW MEXICO TERRITORY

INDIAN TERRITORY

ARKANSAS

TENNESSEE

NORTH CAROLINA

SOUTH CAROLINA

MISSISSIPPI

ALABAMA

GEORGIA

TEXAS

LOUISIANA

FLORIDA

N

0   400 km
0   400 miles

The slaves Dred and Harriet Scott sued for their freedom in 1846, arguing that their travels in the territories of Minnesota and Wisconsin—north of the Missouri Compromise line—made them free people.

free or slave. When a later draft of the bill divided Nebraska in two, creating a new territory of Kansas, most people assumed Kansas would be opened to slavery. People in the North—many of whom viewed the Missouri Compromise as sacrosanct—were outraged. Almost overnight, people who had never publicly opposed slavery's extension became energized against the Kansas-Nebraska Act. Abolitionists, Free Soilers, Northern Whigs, and many Northern Democrats formed "anti-Nebraska" coalitions, which quickly coalesced into the new Republican Party.

Meanwhile, the race to settle Kansas was on between residents of slave and free states. Pro-slavery Missourians and anti-slavery Northerners clashed violently in several battles that became known as "Bleeding Kansas." After pro-slavery "border ruffians" sacked the free-state town of Lawrence, a wild-eyed abolitionist named John Brown retaliated by murdering five pro-slavery Kansans in May 1856. Kansas became, for both the Northerners and the Southerners, a powerful symbol of sectional strife.

Dred Scott Decision

With "Bleeding Kansas" threatening to draw the entire nation into open warfare, the U.S. Supreme Court decided to settle the question of slavery in the territories once and for all. The Court's justices—five of whom were Southern slaveholders—decided to rule on the case of a slave named Dred Scott in 1857.

Scott's owner, an army doctor from Missouri, had taken his slave with him to military posts in Illinois and Wisconsin Territory (part of which became the state of Minnesota) for several years before returning home. Scott sued for his freedom when the doctor died, claiming that his prolonged stay in territory north of 36°30' made him a free man. Scott's case made it all the way to the Supreme Court as a test case over whether Congress had the power to ban slavery in the territories.

First, the justices, led by the slaveholder Roger B. Taney of Maryland, declared the Missouri Compromise ban unconstitutional. But they didn't stop there. Congress, they ruled, had no power to keep slavery out of any territory, since slaves were private property. Finally, Taney ruled that the case should never have been heard in the first place, since African Americans were not citizens of the United States and therefore could not sue in court. The decision must have come as a surprise to blacks who were legal citizens in several Northern states and therefore citizens of the United States. Most Northerners were shocked: to them, Taney's decision smacked of racist, sectional politics. But the abolitionist editor and ex-slave Frederick Douglass expressed optimism: "We, the abolitionists and colored people, should meet this decision, unlooked for and monstrous as it appears, in a cheerful spirit," he wrote. "This very attempt to blot out forever the hopes of an enslaved people may be one necessary link in the chain of events preparatory to the complete overthrow of the whole slave system."

Dred Scott decision, 1857

free state

slave state

open to slavery by decision

slavery exists but not subject to standard territorial sovereignty

Dred Scott's travel route

Runaways, Kidnappings, and Abolitionists

The Underground Railroad

Far more slaves ran away than engaged in open rebellion. A large majority were captured and returned to their owners. As the 19th century wore on, however, black and white opponents of slavery constructed a large network to assist fugitives in their escapes to freedom. Taken altogether, this network became known as the "Underground Railroad."

Many of the stories about the Underground Railroad are more myth than history. There were few or no stations in the South, where most slaves lived, and runaways had to rely on their own ingenuity to make it to the relative safety of the Northern states. And the network of "stations" never achieved the rates of success claimed by hysterical slave owners (during the 1850s only about 1,000 slaves escaped per year—roughly one quarter of 1 percent of the 4 million enslaved blacks).

Harriet Tubman (far left), a runaway slave from Maryland, personally helped as many as 300 enslaved blacks escape to freedom. She was called the "Moses of her people."

Still, the runaway slave Harriet Tubman made 19 separate trips to the South to spirit 300 slaves to freedom. And Levi Coffin, the reputed "president" of the Underground Railroad, reported receiving up to 100 slaves a year at his house in Cincinnati during its days as one of the railroad's major "stations." Estimates suggest that as many as 3,000 blacks and whites at any one time helped about 75,000 slaves find freedom. Favored routes led through communities in Ohio and Pennsylvania with high populations of Quakers (who were often outspoken abolitionists and volunteered their homes and meeting houses) and through cities with significant free black populations like Philadelphia, New York, and Boston.

In addition to aiding in the escape of slaves and giving countless others hope, the Underground Railroad, myths and all, significantly stepped up tensions between North and South. Southerners deeply resented Northern help given to runaways and demanded strict fugitive slave laws and punishment for those caught violating them. This resentment was far out of proportion to the extent of effectiveness of the Underground Railroad itself. On the other side of the Mason-Dixon line, fugitives risking everything for freedom brought Northerners face to face with the cruelties of slavery. Runaways were real people who needed help, not faraway abstractions. The presence

TEX

to Mexico

of slave catchers in Northern cities and towns outraged even people who had never opposed slavery in the South or cared for African Americans.

The growth of an abolitionist movement paralleled the existence of the Underground Railroad, dedicated to immediately ending slavery in the United States. Prominent abolitionists like Sojourner Truth, Henry Highland Garnet, and Frederick Douglass raised money to help runaways, printed anti-slavery petitions and newspapers, went on speaking tours, and lobbied politicians to abolish the institution. Their constant pressure—in the face of legal trouble, violence, and even death threats—kept the issue of slavery at the enter of American politics.

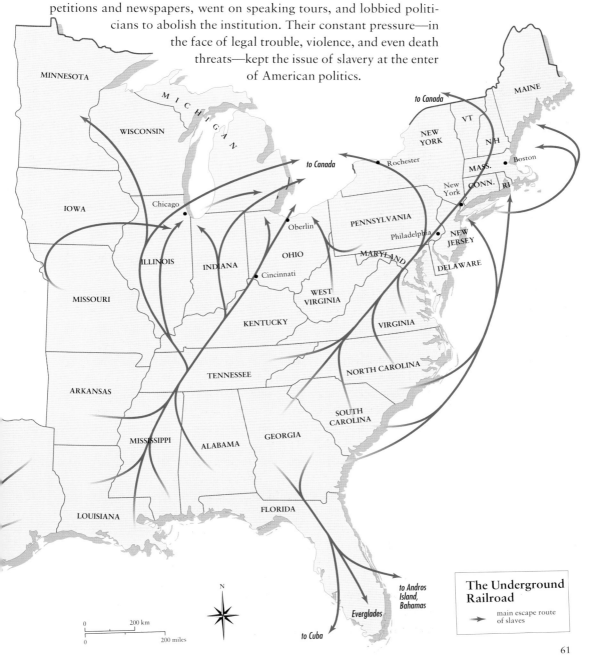

The Underground Railroad

→ main escape route of slaves

Famous Escapes, Kidnappings, and Renditions

This map illustrates how difficult it was for slaves to escape to freedom from the Deep South. Most of the best-known African American escapees—including Frederick Douglass, Harriet Tubman, Henry Highland Garnet, and Josiah Henson—lived in border states. Henry "Box" Brown was actually shipped from Richmond to Philadelphia in a crate by the Adams Express Company. The harrowing escape of William and Ellen Craft from Georgia was a rare exception. Ellen, whose light skin allowed her to pass as white, dressed as a planter, and William accompanied her as the "planter's" trusty slave. The two boldly boarded a train for Savannah near their plantation in Macon, Georgia, and made their way by boat and rail to Philadelphia. Their escape required several things ordinary slaves did not usually possess: money and an intricate knowledge

of transportation networks.

Other famous escapees also tended to have important advantages. Frederick Bailey was a slave on Maryland's Eastern Shore. As a child a kind master taught him the basics of reading, a skill which he developed by tricking local white children into helping him. He also acquired experience and knowledge denied to most slaves as a "hired slave" in cosmopolitan Baltimore. After two failed escapes, Bailey forged the papers of a free black sailor and boarded a steamer for Wilmington, Delaware. With

Famous escapes, kidnappings, and renditions

Kidnappings
- - -▶ Solomon Northrup

Escapes to freedom
──▶ Anthony Burns, 1854
──▶ William and Ellen Craft, 1848
──▶ Frederick Douglass, 1838
──▶ Henry Highland Garnet, 1824
──▶ Josiah Henson, 1830
──▶ Solomon Northrup
──▶ James W.C. Pennington, 1827
──▶ Harriet Tubnam, 1849

Returns to slavery
- - -▶ Anthony Burns, 1854

the aid of other black abolitionists he settled in New Bedford, Massachusetts, and he changed his name to Frederick Douglass to avoid easy detection.

Harriet Tubman, known as the "Moses of her people" for helping as many as 300 slaves escape, and Henry Highland Garnet, a famous black abolitionist, were also from the border state of Maryland, as was James W. C. Pennington. Josiah Henson was a Kentucky plantation slave who escaped with his wife and children by walking through Indiana and Ohio

$150 REWARD

RANAWAY from the subscriber, on the night of the 2d instant, a negro man, who calls himself *Henry May*, about 22 years old, 5 feet 6 or 8 inches high, ordinary color, rather chunky built, bushy head, and has it divided mostly on one side, and keeps it very nicely combed; has been raised in the house, and is a first rate dining-room servant, and was in a tavern in Louisville for 18 months. I expect he is now in Louisville trying to make his escape to a free state, (in all probability to Cincinnati, Ohio.) Perhaps he may try to get employment on a steamboat. He is a good cook, and is handy in any capacity as a house servant. Had on when he left, a dark cassinett coatee, and dark striped cassinett pantaloons, new—he had other clothing. I will give $50 reward if taken in Louisville; 100 dollars if taken one hundred miles from Louisville in this State, and 150 dollars if taken out of this State, and delivered to me, or secured in any jail so that I can get him again. WILLIAM BURKE

Bardstown, Ky., September 3d, 1838.

before boarding a ship for Buffalo, New York, and freedom in Canada. The Hensons were extremely unusual both for their excellent luck and their escape as an intact family.

Unfortunately, the journey North to freedom was sometimes reversed. Free African American Solomon Northrup of Saratoga Springs, New York, was kidnapped and sold into slavery by two unscrupulous whites in 1841. Northrup was later sold in New Orleans to a cotton planter from remote Bayou Boeuf near the Red River in Louisiana. He remained enslaved for 12 years before he met a kind white carpenter who wrote a letter to Northrup's family and friends in New York. Using an 1840 New York law passed at the urging of the state's free blacks to protect citizens from being sold into slavery, Northrup rejoined his family in 1853. The publication of his harrowing tale, along with Douglass's first autobiography, helped persuade Northerners of the evils of slavery.

Even after a successful escape to freedom, runaways needed to maintain constant vigilance against slave catchers, especially after the passage of the Fugitive Slave Law. The law, part of the Compromise of 1850, required only an affidavit from a slave state court identifying an African American as a runaway to return the person to slavery. Fugitives were forbidden to speak in their own defense. In one spectacular case, a Virginia slave named Anthony Burns escaped to Boston in 1854. Apprehended by a federal marshal, Burns's case became a cause célèbre as angry abolitionists tried to rescue him and block his return to slavery. Thousands of Bostonians somberly lined the streets as Burns was marched by soldiers and marines to the harbor and returned to bondage. Abolitionists purchased his freedom the following year, and Burns died a free man in Canada.

Running away was one of the most common ways slaves rebelled against their condition. Although a large majority of runaways were eventually caught, some fugitives (usually those from the border states) gained freedom in the North or in Canada.

Slavery and the Civil War

Slave "Contraband" Camps, 1861–63

After the early battles of the Civil War, it was clear that the Union would not win a quick victory against the Confederacy. As the war intensified, Union commanders and leaders were faced with a different challenge: everywhere the Northern army advanced, runaway slaves (seeing it as an army of liberation) streamed behind Union lines. Hundreds and then thousands of slaves "voted with their feet" for liberty and left plantations and farms for places occupied by Union soldiers including southeastern Louisiana, Missouri, Tennessee, Virginia, and the coastal Carolinas.

At the beginning of the war, President Lincoln instructed his generals to return the slaves to their masters, insisting the Civil War was about preserving the Union, not freeing the slaves. As the war progressed, however, and the South continued to win battles, Northern military planners began to see the need for "total war": warfare designed to utilize every resource that would bring victory. This included the use of any tactic—even destruction of property or institutions — that would damage the enemy's "will to fight." An attack on slavery, some argued, would strike at the heart of the Confederacy's African American labor force and invest the war with a new moral cause: fighting for freedom.

As early as 1861, runaway slaves forced Union generals to see them as a potential resource. Generals like Benjamin Butler, whose army had penetrated into Virginia, refused to return runaways to their owners and began to use them as laborers and even soldiers. He insisted they were "contraband of war," and should be utilized for the cause.

Lincoln was furious: he

Slave "contrabands" camps, 1861–63

- Union state/territory
- Confederate state/territory
- under Union control, 1861–63
- Contraband camp

was still unwilling to make the war a fight for freedom. Abolitionists fumed. "To fight against slaveholders, without fighting against slavery," said Frederick Douglass, "is a half-hearted business, and paralyzes the hands engaged in it. . . . War for the destruction of liberty must be met with war for the destruction of slavery." But the slaves' action and Butler's response forced the government to compromise. In 1862, Congress passed the Contraband Act, classifying runaway slaves as contraband of war. Instead of returning runaways to their masters, they were placed in internment camps, where they were forbidden to aid the Union Army as soldiers or laborers. Northern religious and social groups led by free blacks were horrified when they visited the contraband camps, and lobbied strenuously for their dismantling.

For the rest of the war slaves who came within Union lines were known as contrabands. Their dramatic act—"freeing" themselves—helped force Lincoln and Congress to transform a war to preserve the Union into one for emancipation.

The Emancipation Proclamation

It was a dire military situation that drove Lincoln to alter his policy on emancipation. Although morally opposed to slavery, Lincoln was faced with the daunting task of keeping the loyal slave states of Missouri, Maryland, and Kentucky in the Union. A general emancipation proclamation would have handed the border states to the secessionists. But pressure from African Americans, his military leaders, and his own political party compelled Lincoln to move toward emancipation.

General Ulysses Grant believed that if the South could not "be whipped in any way other than through a war against slavery, let it come to that." This belief, compounded by Confederate success on the battlefield, forced Lincoln's hand. On July 13, 1862, Lincoln told his secretary of the Navy he intended to issue an emancipation proclamation. "We must free the slaves or ourselves be subdued," he said. "The Administration must set an example, and strike at the heart of the rebellion." The president decided to delay the proclamation until a Union victory in the field, so as not to appear desperate. The proclamation, which would affect the lives of millions of African Americans, languished for two long months in a desk drawer while Lincoln waited for good news from the battlefield.

It came on September 17, when the Battle of Antietam in Maryland ended in a draw. Lincoln retrieved his proclamation and on September 22 proclaimed that if any state (or part of a state) was still in rebellion on January 1, 1863, the slaves there would be "forever free." When the deadline arrived no Southern state had re-entered the Union, and slaves in the border states, of course, were unaffected by the proclamation. Lincoln's edict, therefore, failed to free a single slave. It did, however, set in motion the events that would bring about the legal abolition of slavery for 4 million African Americans. If the Confederacy died as a result of the war, slavery would die along with it.

Radical Reconstruction, 1866–77

African Americans, who constituted a majority in South Carolina, wielded considerable power in the state legislature during Reconstruction. In the state's first legislative session after readmission, blacks held a 2-1 majority in the House.

In his famous address at Gettysburg, Abraham Lincoln said the Union could be reconstructed only by experiencing a "new birth of freedom." For the nation's African Americans, this meant significantly more than the abolition of slavery. Black abolitionists like Frederick Douglass had long argued that freedom meant more than simply "owning" oneself: it meant African Americans had to be treated as equals to whites before the law, and that they should be allowed to vote in order to protect those rights. But many Southerners—joined by significant numbers of Northerners—were unwilling to grant blacks equal rights.

After Lincoln was assassinated in April 1865, his Tennessee-born vice president, Andrew Johnson, assumed the nation's highest office. Johnson quickly proposed to exclude African Americans completely from the Reconstruction process, saying that "white men alone must govern the South." After a delegation led by Douglass confronted Johnson on black suffrage, he told his secretary that "those damned sons of bitches thought they had me in a trap!...[T]hat damned Douglass, he's just like any nigger, and he would sooner cut a white man's throat than not." African Americans and radical Republicans were outraged when the Southern states ratified their new constitutions without enfranchising a single black man. Enfranchising women of any race was not on the agenda of most politicians in either North or South.

Things got worse in the fall of 1865 when some Southern states enacted "Black Codes" that reduced freed people to slavery-like conditions. Congress, controlled by Radical Republicans, took matters into their own hands. They began impeachment proceedings against Johnson and passed the 14th and 15th Amendments, which granted African Americans full citizenship and gave black men the right to vote. Then they divided the South into five military districts, each with a military governor, and forced the states to write new constitutions which included the 13th, 14th, and 15th Amendments.

With Union soldiers occupying the region and black men given the right to vote, large numbers of African Americans were elected to help rewrite the state constitutions. Blacks and their white Unionist and Northern allies organized Union leagues to mobilize new black voters for the Republican Party; by September 1867 there were 735,000 black voters and only 635,000 white voters in the ten Southern states. The new state constitutions enacted universal male suffrage (putting them ahead of many Northern states), mandated statewide public schools for blacks and whites, and increased the states' responsibility for social welfare.

With African Americans representing almost 80 percent of Southern Republicans, black men were elected to 15–20 percent of the public offices. Fourteen African Americans were elected to the House of Representatives and two to the Senate between 1868 and 1876. African Americans wielded the greatest influence in South Carolina, where they constituted a majority of the population. In the first legislature after the state was readmitted to the Union, there were 87 blacks and 40 whites. Between 1868 and 1896 Louisiana had 133 black legislators, including 38 state senators. Three African Americans—P.B.S. Pinchback, Oscar Dunn, and C. C. Antoine—served as lieutenant governor, and Pinchback was acting governor for 43 days in 1873 when the governor was removed from office. Yet at no time did blacks control a state government.

A large majority of black elected officials were well educated, but racist Democrats chafed under what they called "Negro rule." Venal and racist propaganda claimed that all black voters and officeholders were illiterate and incompetent—a lie that was later enshrined in folk memory and history books. The fact remains that both blacks and poor Southern whites benefited greatly from Radical Reconstruction. By 1877, Northern Republicans had grown exhausted from enforcing Reconstruction, and Southern conservatives, acting through terror and propaganda, regained control of the state governments. One by one the Southern states rolled back the gains made by blacks, reinstating poll taxes, literacy tests, and property requirements to disfranchise black citizens. In the decades to come, freed slaves and their descendants suffered second-class citizenship and brutal repression at the hands of Southern whites.

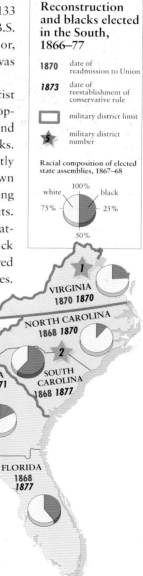

Radical Reconstruction and blacks elected in the South, 1866–77

1870   date of readmission to Union

1873   date of reestablishment of conservative rule

☐   military district limit

★ 5   military district number

Racial composition of elected state assemblies, 1867–68

white   100%   black
75%   25%
50%

VIRGINIA 1870 1870

NORTH CAROLINA 1868 1870

ARKANSAS 1868 1874

TENNESSEE 1866 1869 (Restored to the Union before Radical Reconstruction)

SOUTH CAROLINA 1868 1877

TEXAS 1871 1873

ALABAMA 1868 1874

GEORGIA 1870 1871

MISSISSIPPI 1870 1876

LOUISIANA 1868 1877

FLORIDA 1868 1877

0   200 km
0   200 miles

N

"Exodusters"

After federal troops pulled out of the South and Reconstruction collapsed, thousands of Southern blacks decided the time was right to move. With ex-Confederates back in power in most states and hate groups such as the Ku Klux Klan terrorizing the countryside, many African Americans found life in the post-Reconstruction South unbearable. Some, like Henry McNeal Turner, encouraged blacks to leave the country and move to Africa; few African Americans, however, were willing to leave the country that was the only home they knew. Far more significant was the exodus of blacks from the rural South to the North and West after Reconstruction.

Right: Emigrants from the Deep South waiting for a Mississippi River boat in the 1880s. Blacks hoping for a better life in Kansas and the West became known as "Exodusters" after the biblical exodus from Egypt.

Thousands of ex-slaves answered the call sounded by Benjamin "Pap" Singleton, a minister from Tennessee, to abandon the racial prejudice of the South and go West. Singleton issued circulars like "The Advantage of Living in a Free State," encouraging blacks to follow him to Kansas. In a time where their political rights were being trampled, lynchings were on the rise, and economic depressions made sharecropping and tenant farming resemble slavery, some Southern blacks decided they had no future in the South. The largest organized exodus to Kansas began in Nashville in 1880, where more than 60,000 unhappy blacks gathered to begin a journey to a new life. Singleton's followers were quickly dubbed "Exodusters" by newspapers that compared their flight from the South with the Israelites flight from Egyptian slavery.

The movement continued in the 1880s, as black leaders like David Turner in Oklahoma, Edward McCabe in Kansas, and Allen Allensworth in California established and promoted politically independent and economically viable all-black towns. Many of these settlements were victims of white racism, poor planning, and bad luck, but others, like Nicodemus, a town named for an African slave in western Kansas, took root. A flier inviting African Americans to settle in Nicodemus included a song, with the chorus:

> Good time coming, good time coming,
> Long, long time on the way;
> Run and tell Elijah to hurry up Pomp,
> To meet us under the cottonwood tree,
> In the great Solomon Valley
> At the first break of day.

The Exodusters experienced resistance from other blacks, including Booker T. Washington, who urged those weighing flight to "cast your bucket down where you are." The Exodusters were the first mass movement of blacks after the Civil War, but they would be joined in the 20th century by millions of others fleeing the South for a better life in the North, West, and Midwest.

The "Exodusters"

state abandoned by
black Exodusters

★ departure point,
1880

→ exodus route

Western state which
attracted blacks

● city which attracted
black migrants

PART IV: AFRICAN AMERICANS UNDER ARMS

This is our golden opportunity. Let us accept it, and forever wipe out the dark reproaches unsparingly hurled against us by our enemies. Let us win for ourselves the gratitude of our country, and the best blessings of our posterity through all time.
—Frederick Douglass, 1863

Africans and African Americans have fought bravely in every major military action since colonial times, despite the fact that black soldiers and sailors were forced to battle twin foes: the wartime enemy and withering racism both inside and outside the armed services. Inside the military, blacks were routinely ordered to perform dangerous missions or relegated to auxiliary duties like building roads or burying the dead. They were effectively barred from serving in any military branch besides the army until World War II. And after each war ended blacks repeatedly returned to a larger society that minimized their military contributions and confined them to second-class status. Yet with every armed conflict, African Americans clung to a belief that military service in wartime represented a clear path toward greater freedom and opportunity, for the individual as well as the race as a whole.

The 107th Colored Infantry, photographed at Fort Corcoran, part of the Union defensive perimeter around Washington D.C. during the Civil War.

The Revolutionary War set several precedents for black military service. Africans and African Americans fighting on both sides saw military service as a means by which a slave might win his freedom or a free black improve his standing in the community. Yet, in what would become a pattern in later conflicts, only a relative few blacks were able to take advantage of the war to improve their status. After the war ended, those slaves who sided with the British were either returned to their masters or evacuated to Nova Scotia and Sierra Leone. Northern black soldiers fared slightly better, and their brave service in battles like Bunker Hill and Saratoga helped convince leaders in several states to formally abolish slavery in the years after the Revolution.

Far more significant for African Americans was the Civil War, known to many blacks as the Jubilee War. Seeing the war's potential to become a war for freedom, blacks were among the first to volunteer for service in the Union Army in 1861. But President Lincoln, seeking to mollify the border states that remained in the Union, refused them until early 1863. That year saw the formation of several all-black regiments, although at the time they were paid less than white soldiers and generally served only as labor battalions and garrison forces. Black troops won the right to fight in combat, however, helping to destroy slavery and the Confederacy and giving the United States a new birth of freedom at the war's conclusion. More than 186,000 African Americans served in the Union Army in the war.

After the Civil War the U.S. government kept several black regiments active, ordering most of them to the West to fight Indians and protect American business interests there. These same Buffalo Soldier units also saw action in the Spanish-American War, in both Cuba and the Philippines. More than a few black soldiers and sailors (and black leaders at home) drew parallels between American imperialism abroad and its treatment of racial minorities at home. Segregated black troops were also a vital part of the U.S. forces that turned the tide for the allies during World War I. Racism was rampant on every level and especially visible in the lily-white officers' corps and harrowing race riots on military bases. Still, all-black units like the Harlem Hell Fighters of the 369th and the Tenth Cavalry fought bravely on the Western Front, halting the German advance and pushing them all the way back to the Rhine in 1918.

World War II struck many African Americans as an ideal opportunity to make gains at home by fighting racism and injustice abroad. The Axis powers included Nazi Germany, where Hitler had come to power preaching racism and anti-Semitism, and Italy, which had invaded the black kingdom of Ethiopia in 1935. Black leaders spoke of a "Double-V Campaign" for twin victories against racial injustice in Europe and in the United States. Approximately 1 million blacks served in the armed services, filling out the ranks in he Marine Corps, Navy, and Coast Guard, which had long been closed off to them. The age of the segregated military came to an end in 1948, when President Harry S Truman issued an executive order integrating all branches of the armed forces. Thus the Korean War (1950–53) was the first armed conflict where African American and white troops fought together side by side.

America's involvement in Vietnam closely paralleled the struggles of the civil rights movement. A larger percentage of the nation's African Americans fought—and died—in the war than the nation's whites, a statistic that added to the racial tumult of the 1960s. When federal troops were called in to quell riots in Detroit in 1967, many saw disturbing parallels between action in Vietnam and in urban America. Blacks continued to volunteer for and serve in the army nonetheless, and many veterans were sorely disappointed at the treatment they received after the United States pulled out. Since Vietnam the United States has deployed its armed forces in several limited engagements including the Persian Gulf War, peacekeeping and humanitarian missions in Haiti and Somalia, and in the Balkans.

Ironically, the U.S. armed forces—the nation's most authoritarian institution—has been more successful than the private sector in implementing integration. African Americans have risen to the military's highest ranks, and occupy positions of authority in numbers that far outpace those in the rest of society. Yet patterns of racism and inequality established hundreds of years ago persist.

Black Patriots and Loyalists

African Americans and the Revolution, 1770–81

The revolutionary spirit following the imperial crisis with Great Britain was not confined to whites. The revolutionary writings of Jefferson, Jean-Jacques Rousseau, and Tom Paine were read and discussed by hundreds of thousands of colonists in the 1760s and '70s, black as well as white, free as well as slave. Many were more than willing to take up arms for the revolutionary cause.

Even before the formal outbreak of hostilities in 1775, blacks were willing to risk their lives to resist British encroachments. A runaway slave named Crispus Attucks, a vehement opponent of British policies including the occupation of Boston in 1770, was one of five protestors gunned down in the Boston Massacre. And as early as the battles of Lexington and Concord, blacks took up arms against British soldiers. Blacks' brave service in these early battles brought a vexing question before the patriot leaders: should blacks be armed to fight against Great Britain? After the Stono rebellion, fear of slave insurrections even in New England led colonists to bar blacks from owning guns and serving in militias. Thus the Committee on Safety ruled that only freemen could be used in the war.

There is ample evidence, however, that the committee's ruling was ignored: enslaved blacks joined their free brethren in the Battle of Bunker Hill, and some slaves were freed explicitly so they could serve in the army. Among those who were commended for service in the war were Prince Hall (a black activist who later established the first black Masonic hall), Cato Tufts, Titus Colburn, and Cuff Hayes.

Still, there was widespread opposition in both North and South to a major black presence in the Continental Army. When George Washington took command in mid-1775, his war council instructed recruiters not to enlist any new black soldiers; an order later that year rejected blacks altogether—dubious thanks for black participation in battles like Bunker Hill.

All this changed in November 1775 when Lord Dunmore, the royal governor of Virginia and a British loyalist, declared "all indentured servants, Negroes, or others . . . free, that they are able and willing to bear arms, they joining his Majesty's troops." Later that month Virginia militiamen defeated a force of almost 800 slaves and 200 redcoats; most of the slaves fell prey to smallpox after the battle. Not surprisingly, thousands of slaves ran away toward British lines to seek the freedom denied them during the previous century and a half (Thomas Jefferson estimated that 30,000 Virginia slaves ran away in 1778 alone). Southern slaves viewed the British troops as an army of emancipation, not invasion.

The next month, due to Dunmore's decree and protests led by Prince Hall, Washington reversed his policy and allowed free blacks to serve in the Continental Army. Washington also cited fears that blacks would seek to fight on the British side if not permitted to serve with the patriots. Approximately 5,000 blacks eventually served in the Continental Army, most of them from the

North. And although there were a few all-black companies (including the Bucks of America in Massachusetts), a large majority of black soldiers fought in groups composed largely of white men. At least some black soldiers participated in nearly every one of the major battles of the Revolution, including Ticonderoga, Princeton, Brandywine, Savannah, and Yorktown.

Resettlement of Black Loyalists after the Revolution

Although 5,000 blacks fought with the patriots in the Revolution, most enslaved African Americans concluded their best chance for liberty lay with the British army. According to historians, almost 10 percent of slaves—more than 50,000—ran away during the war. Of these,

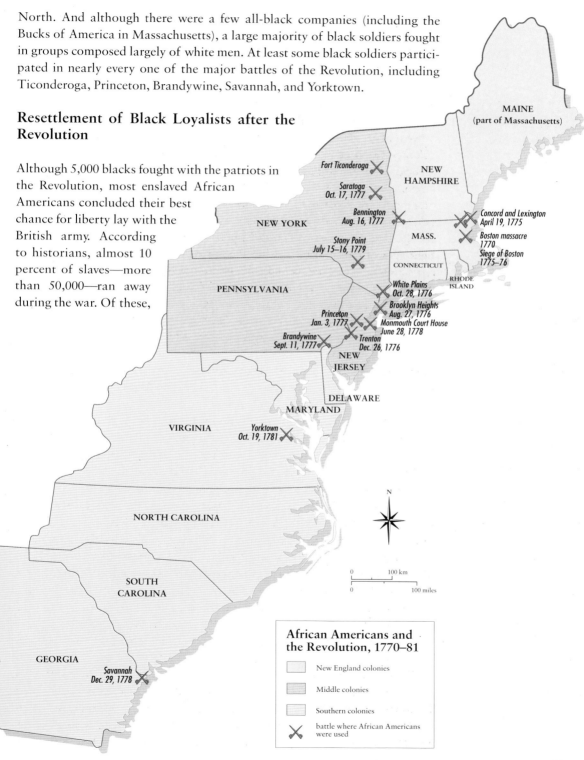

MAINE
(part of Massachusetts)

Fort Ticonderoga

NEW HAMPSHIRE

Saratoga
Oct. 17, 1777

NEW YORK

Bennington
Aug. 16, 1777

Concord and Lexington
April 19, 1775

Stony Point
July 15–16, 1779

MASS.

Boston massacre
1770
Siege of Boston
1775–76

CONNECTICUT

RHODE ISLAND

PENNSYLVANIA

White Plains
Oct. 28, 1776

Brooklyn Heights
Aug. 27, 1776

Princeton
Jan. 3, 1777

Monmouth Court House
June 28, 1778

Brandywine
Sept. 11, 1777

Trenton
Dec. 26, 1776

NEW JERSEY

DELAWARE

MARYLAND

VIRGINIA

Yorktown
Oct. 19, 1781

NORTH CAROLINA

N

SOUTH CAROLINA

0   100 km
0   100 miles

GEORGIA

Savannah
Dec. 29, 1778

African Americans and the Revolution, 1770–81

New England colonies

Middle colonies

Southern colonies

battle where African Americans were used

73

approximately 20,000 were evacuated by the British. At least 6,000 loyalist blacks departed from Charleston, 4,000 from Savannah, and more than 3,000 from New York City.

Some runaway loyalists were quickly disappointed with Great Britain: many were treated as contraband and faced resale to new (loyalist) planters; others ran away only to face punishment by their owners when the redcoats failed to rescue them. But, for the most part, reaching British lines meant freedom for runaway slaves. When redcoat troops began their withdrawal after Yorktown, they took blacks with them. If they had served in the British army or navy, they were allowed passage to any part of the British Empire. Some chose to go to Jamaica or London, but most went to Halifax, Nova Scotia, where the British government promised to care for the refugees.

Most Nova Scotians did not welcome the new arrivals, however, and the British treated them with neglect. These people had arrived in Canada with nothing: no possessions, no kinship ties, no familiarity with the climate or landscape. In 1792 Thomas Peters, a black leader in Halifax, traveled to London to plead the refugees' case. As a result of Peters's visit, the British created a new colony for ex-slaves in Sierra Leone, on West Africa's Rice Coast. Not surprisingly, they christened their new home Freetown. Theirs was the first African state founded and controlled by blacks from what is now the United States.

More than 10,000 blacks fought in the Revolutionary War, on both sides of the conflict. Most enslaved blacks saw the British army, which promised to free each slave who volunteered, as one of liberation, not tyranny.

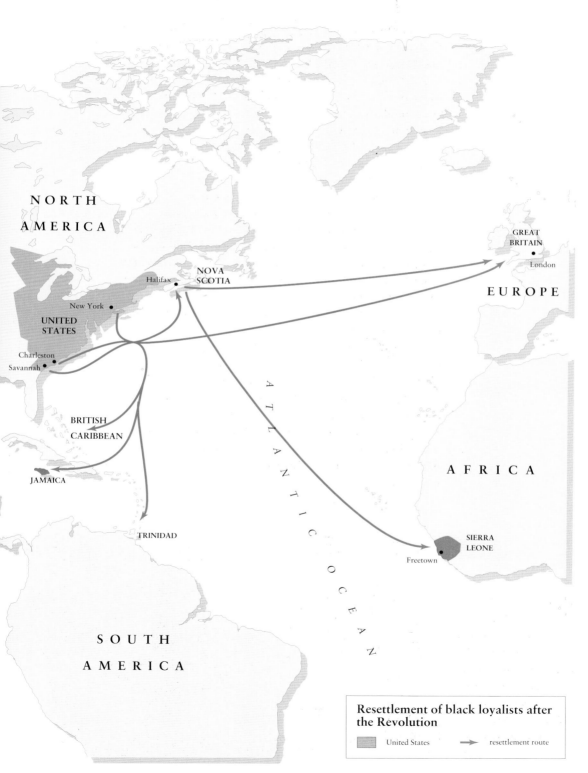

NORTH
AMERICA

GREAT
BRITAIN
●
London

NOVA
SCOTIA

Halifax ●

EUROPE

New York ●

UNITED
STATES

Charleston ●
Savannah ●

ATLANTIC

BRITISH
CARIBBEAN

AFRICA

JAMAICA

SIERRA
LEONE

Freetown ●

TRINIDAD

OCEAN

SOUTH
AMERICA

Resettlement of black loyalists after the Revolution

United States   → resettlement route

Black Men in Blue

African Americans, with an eye to the Civil War's potential to become a war for freedom, were among the first to volunteer to serve in the Union Army in 1861. But a law dating from 1812 barred blacks from service in the U.S. military, and President Lincoln and others still held that the Civil War was a conflict between whites over the fate of the Union. Those opposed to African American enlistment clearly understood that one consequence of blacks' fighting for the Union would be a major step toward racial equality. So, too, did abolitionists like Frederick Douglass. "Once let the black man get upon his person the brass letters, U.S.," he said, "and a musket on his shoulder and bullets in his pocket, and there is no power on earth which can deny that he has earned the right to citizenship." He was right: beginning in 1863, blacks did fight for the Union, helping to destroy slavery and the Confederacy, giving the United States a new birth of freedom after the war was over.

The first African Americans to fight in the Civil War were runaway slaves armed by Union officers in defiance of Lincoln's orders. As early as 1861–62, Union commanders occupying portions of South Carolina and Louisiana began to organize black regiments. But the U.S. government, hoping to strike at the heart of the Confederacy and make up for a lag in white enlistment, didn't lift the ban on African American troops until 1863. When first organized, the new black regiments were paid less than whites, their officers were white, and they served only as labor battalions and garrison forces. Over the next year, however, black soldiers won the right to fight, earn equal pay, and, in rare cases, be led by African American officers.

Black leaders like Frederick Douglass served as recruiting agents, and massive rallies in New York, Boston, and Philadelphia helped spur 186,000 blacks to enlist by the end of the war. Once in combat, black soldiers quickly quashed the racist notion that they wouldn't fight as well as whites. Eight black regiments participated in the assault on Port Hudson in Louisiana, and others bravely defended a Union outpost near Vicksburg called Milliken's Bend. Perhaps most significant was the 54th Massachusetts Infantry, the first black regiment raised in the North. Two of Frederick Douglass's sons were in the regiment, one as sergeant major, and the commanding officer was Robert Gould Shaw, the scion of a prominent abolitionist family. After months of garrisoning forts and supplying white soldiers, the 54th finally won the right to fight on July 18,

Fort Wagner, South Carolina, July 18, 1863

→ attack of 54th Massachusetts

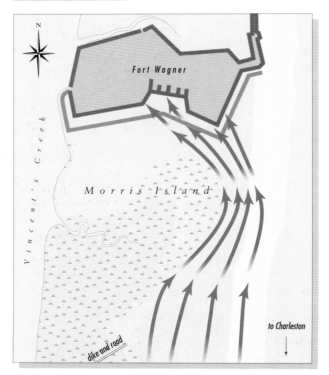

1863. The regiment was assigned the lead position in an assault on Fort Wagner, part of the network of defenses fortifying Charleston, South Carolina. The assault was a bloody one, and the black soldiers were repelled with 50 percent casualties. But every witness saw the 54th Massachusetts fight with tremendous courage. According to the *New York Tribune*, the battle "made Fort Wagner a name to the colored race as Bunker Hill had been for ninety years to the white Yankees."

The Confederate government reacted to the use of African American troops by declaring that they would take no black prisoners. Unlike white troops, blacks in uniform were often massacred as they surrendered, most famously at Fort Pillow in Tennessee. Despite this knowledge, African Americans continued to volunteer for service and fight with astonishing courage in more than 200 battles across the South. More than 38,000 black soldiers lost their lives during the war, a rate of mortality nearly 40 percent higher than that for white troops. Much of this can be attributed to the "take no prisoners" policy practiced by Southerners in dealing with black soldiers.

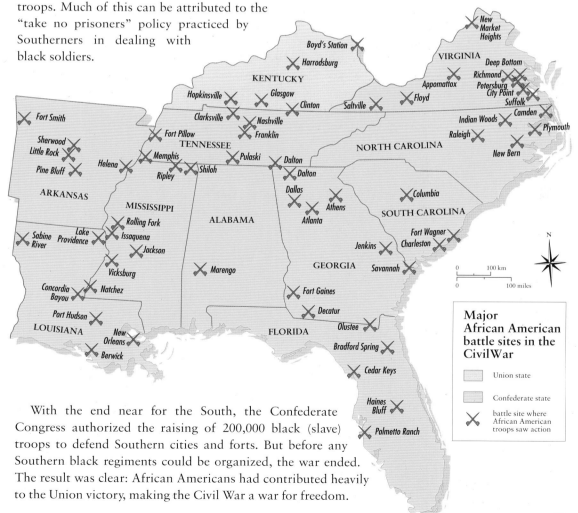

Major African American battle sites in the Civil War

Union state

Confederate state

✕ battle site where African American troops saw action

With the end near for the South, the Confederate Congress authorized the raising of 200,000 black (slave) troops to defend Southern cities and forts. But before any Southern black regiments could be organized, the war ended. The result was clear: African Americans had contributed heavily to the Union victory, making the Civil War a war for freedom.

Buffalo Soldiers and the Indian Wars, 1866–90

Black soldiers proved beyond a shadow of a doubt that they could fight with courage and cunning during the Civil War. After the South surrendered in 1865, the U.S. army quickly focused on protecting white settlement and business interests in the far West. White settlers had followed the transcontinental railroad lines into Indian country, and the region's native inhabitants responded with a series of attacks on towns and rail lines. Those troops not being used to occupy the South, including scores of African American veterans, were quickly diverted to the West.

Blacks had been involved—often against their will—in the struggle between whites and Indians since the first Africans arrived in Virginia in 1619. Knowing they would only inflame hostility in the South, Congress decided to send the best African American army veterans west to fight Plains Indians in 1866. On July 28, Congress authorized the establishment of four permanent black units: two infantry regiments (the U.S. 24th and 25th) and two cavalry regiments (the Ninth and Tenth). Between 1866 and 1880 these four units were engaged almost constantly with recalcitrant Indian tribes. Troops in all four regiments were respectfully nicknamed "Buffalo Soldiers" by their Indian enemies, who saw a resemblance between the hair of the black cavalrymen and the hair of the buffalo, an animal they considered sacred.

The Buffalo Soldiers were involved in countless campaigns against the Sioux, Cheyenne, Crow, Comanche, Arapaho, Navajo, and Apache. They were often the first troops called in to put down rebellions on reservations and face the most fearsome Indian warriors, including Geronimo and Crazy Horse. The regimental officers, who were white, later recalled it was not uncommon for black troops to do virtually all the fighting and sustain nearly all

WASHI
TERRI

OREGON

Ft. Clark

Presidio
of San
Francisco

CALIF

African American soldiers sent to the West to fight Indians after the Civil War were nicknamed "Buffalo Soldiers" by their adversaries.

the casualties, while white troops received the commendations. The Buffalo Soldiers were also used to police Indian Territory (present-day Oklahoma) until 1901, protecting ranchers and cattle from Indian attacks and protecting Indians from land-hungry white settlers. Many Buffalo Soldiers enlisted because they believed their service would help advance their race in other areas of American society. Yet many were sorely disappointed, despite their distinguished service (17 African Americans received the Congressional Medal of Honor during the Indian wars) and the numerous hardships they experienced compared to their white counterparts.

The Buffalo Soldiers and the Indian wars, 1866–90

- area where Buffalo Soldiers served during the Indian wars
- area policed by Buffalo Soldiers before the 1901 Land Rush
- fort housing black troops
- battle

Imperial Wars, 1898–1902

The Buffalo Soldiers of the Ninth and Tenth cavalries and the 24th and 25th infantries also saw service in the Spanish-American War, a conflict that established the United States as an imperial power. The black troops joined thousands of others in Cuba, then a Spanish colony, after the USS Maine sank under mysterious circumstances in February 1898.

Called "Smoked Yankees" by the Spanish because of their dark skin, African American soldiers fought at El Caney, Kettle Hill, Las Guásimas, and in the famous battle of San Juan Hill. There, the Ninth Cavalry's "K" Troop achieved fame and respect for saving Teddy Roosevelt and his Rough Riders, who had become bogged down at the foot of San Juan Hill. Amid chaos, black and white troops intermingled in the charge up the hill, which was successful. Militia regiments from Illinois and Kansas, composed of African Americans from the colonel in command to the lowliest private, helped garrison Cuba and the island of Puerto Rico.

Some African Americans questioned whether black citizens, whose own rights were being whittled away by Jim Crow laws, should support a war to bring American-style "freedom" to Cuba and its significant black population. Henry Turner, the senior bishop of the AME church, put it bluntly: "Negroes who are not disloyal to the United States ought to be lynched." Others disagreed, hoping that black participation in the war would spark a new era of comradeship and good feeling among the races at home. As for the black soldiers, most welcomed the prospect of adventure, a steady salary, and an opportunity to prove themselves as warriors.

Black troops also participated in the naval assault of Manila Bay in the Philippines, a Spanish colony in the Pacific. John Jordan, a black gunner's mate, was in charge of the crew that fired the first shot in the short and successful battle. To the Filipino insurgents, however, the Americans who quickly occupied the islands were little different than their Spanish oppressors. Following the short war, members of the 24th and 25th infantries were stationed in the Philippines and Hawaii, where they witnessed (and participated in) some of the atrocities against and mistreatment of the Filipinos who rebelled against American rule. They also experienced poor treatment by white American soldiers. A very

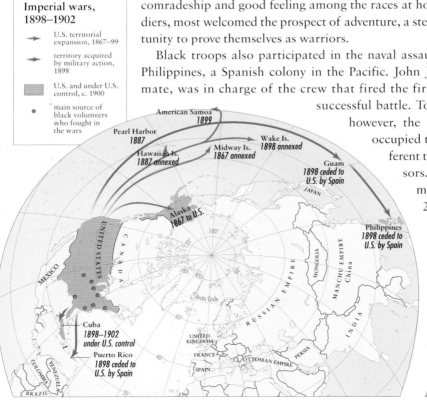

Imperial wars, 1898–1902

→ U.S. territorial expansion, 1867–99

→ territory acquired by military action, 1898

▨ U.S. and under U.S. control, c. 1900

● main source of black volunteers who fought in the wars

American Samoa
1899

Pearl Harbor
1887

Wake Is.
1898 annexed

Midway Is.
1867 annexed

Hawaiian Is.
1887 annexed

Guam
1898 ceded to U.S. by Spain

Alaska
1867 to U.S.

Philippines
1898 ceded to U.S. by Spain

UNITED STATES

CANADA

MEXICO

Cuba
1898–1902 under U.S. control

Puerto Rico
1898 ceded to U.S. by Spain

COLOMBIA

VENEZUELA

BRAZIL

JAPAN

MONGOLIA

MANCHU EMPIRE
China

RUSSIAN EMPIRE

INDIA

UNITED KINGDOM

FRANCE

SPAIN

OTTOMAN EMPIRE

PERSIA

Arctic Circle

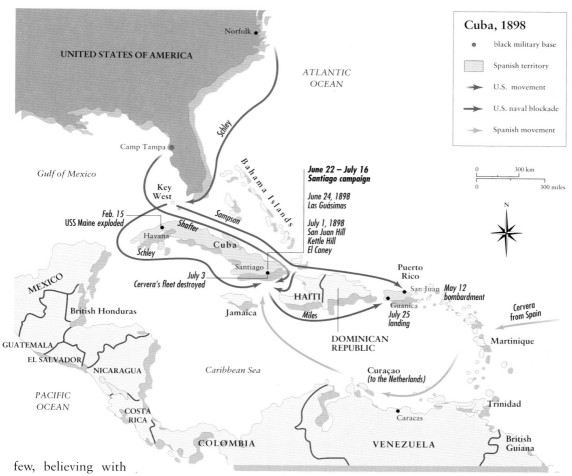

Cuba, 1898

- ● black military base
- Spanish territory
- → U.S. movement
- → U.S. naval blockade
- → Spanish movement

Norfolk ●

UNITED STATES OF AMERICA

ATLANTIC OCEAN

Schley

Camp Tampa ●

Gulf of Mexico

Key West

Feb. 15
USS Maine exploded

Shafter

Havana

Schley

Sampson

Bahama Islands

**June 22 – July 16
Santiago campaign**

June 24, 1898
Las Guásimas

July 1, 1898
San Juan Hill
Kettle Hill
El Caney

Cuba

July 3
Cervera's fleet destroyed

Santiago

HAITI

Miles

Jamaica

MEXICO

British Honduras

GUATEMALA

EL SALVADOR

NICARAGUA

Caribbean Sea

PACIFIC OCEAN

COSTA RICA

COLOMBIA

DOMINICAN REPUBLIC

Puerto Rico

San Juan   May 12
bombardment

Guanica
July 25
landing

Curaçao
(to the Netherlands)

Caracas

VENEZUELA

Cervera
from Spain

Martinique

Trinidad

British Guiana

0   300 km
0   300 miles

N

few, believing with Bishop Turner that the American occupation constituted an "unholy war of conquest," mutinied and cast their lot with the Filipino rebels. Even those that didn't, like veteran John Calloway of the 24th, recalled being "haunted by the feeling of how wrong morally Americans are in their present affair." Turner's and Calloway's solidarity with oppressed Asians would reverberate across the 20th century, climaxing in the 1960s with the widespread view in the black community that both the Vietnamese and African Americans were victims of white oppression.

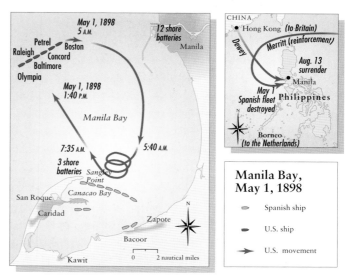

May 1, 1898
5 A.M.

Petrel   Boston
Raleigh   Concord
Baltimore
Olympia

12 shore batteries
Manila

May 1, 1898
1:40 P.M.

Manila Bay

7:35 A.M.

5:40 A.M.

3 shore batteries   Sangley Point

San Roque   Canacao Bay

Caridad

Zapote

Bacoor

Kawit

0   2 nautical miles

N

CHINA
● Hong Kong (to Britain)

Dewey

Merritt (reinforcement)

Aug. 13
surrender

Manila

May 1
Spanish fleet   Philippines
destroyed

N

Borneo
(to the Netherlands)

Manila Bay, May 1, 1898

- Spanish ship
- U.S. ship
- → U.S. movement

World War I

More than 400,000 African Americans served in the U.S. Army during World War I, despite unprecedented racial oppression inside and outside the armed services. During the years between the Philippine insurrection and the U.S. entry into World War I, black mutinies and riots broke out near bases in Brownsville and Houston. Many black elites hoped that the willingness of African Americans to fight in World War I would somehow break the cycle of white repression and black violence. W.E.B. DuBois, a founder of the NAACP, urged his fellow African Americans "to forget our special grievances and close our ranks shoulder to shoulder with our fellow white citizens and the allied nations that are fighting for democracy."

Almost all the blacks who served in the war did so in the U.S. Army, since they were barred from the Marines and Coast Guard and effectively barred from the Navy. In the army they were forced into service units like the stevedores, the quartermasters, and the pioneer infantrymen, whose responsibilities included cooking, cleaning, digging latrines, burying the dead, and loading supplies. The early days of the war followed a familiar pattern, with white officers commanding all-black units like the Tenth Cavalry and the 805th Pioneer Regiment,

The all-black 369th Infantry earned the nickname the "Harlem Hell Fighters" for their service in World War I. Their unit was the first to reach the Rhine River after they successfully repelled a German advance.

and the Harlem Hell Fighters of the 369th. But late in 1917, the government began ROTC programs at several historically black colleges and established a segregated officers training school at Fort Des Moines, Iowa. By the time of the armistice in late 1918, more than 639 black officers led troops during some of the war's most significant campaigns.

In June 1917, black troops landed at the mouth of the Somme River and boarded trains for the Western Front's infamous trenches. They were among the first Americans to arrive, and they fought side by side with soldiers from France and African nations like Senegal and Morocco. In March 1918 Germany launched a major offensive aimed at driving the Allies out of their trenches and then seizing France's English Channel ports. With things looking grim, the all-black 369th, under French command, halted the German advance at Cantigny. The all-black units of the 93rd Division stopped German offensives at Château-Thierry and Belleau Wood. And in June 1918 the Harlem Hell Fighters of the 369th again proved their mettle by driving the Germans back at the Argonne Forest and the Meuse River. Fittingly, their unit was the first to reach the Rhine River.

The French were keenly aware of the significant contributions made by African Americans on their behalf, and they granted the Croix de Guerre to the First Battalion of the 92nd Division and three of the four regiments of the 93rd Infantry. Henry Johnson and Needham Roberts of the 369th each received individual Croix de Guerre for heroism. When the black veterans arrived home, they expected to be treated the same way they had in France—as honorable soldiers who commanded respect. Indeed, more than 5,000 black soldiers were wounded and 750 killed in the "war to end all wars." Instead, they found whites still viewed them as second-class citizens. The NAACP's *Crisis* spoke for returning black soldiers when it said, "This country of ours . . . is yet a shameful land. It lynches. . . . It disfranchises its own citizens. . . . It encourages ignorance. . . . It steals from us. . . . It insults us. . . . We return. We return from fighting. We return fighting."

World War I

	German initial advance, 1914
	Paris defensive line, 1914
	stabilized line, 1914–17
	German spring offensive, 1918
	major U.S. attacks

Armistice line, Nov. 11, 1918

	held by Belgian army
	held by British army
	held by French army
	held by U.S. army
	occupation zones, c. 1919

Specific African American actions

- **A** Cantigny, May 28, 1918
  369th Infantry halts the Germans
- **B** 369th Infantry drives the Germans back to the Argonne Forest and Meuse River
- **C** Chateau-Thierry and Belleau Wood, September 26 – October 5, 1918
  All-black 93rd Division stops German offensive

U.S. offensives

- **1** Aisne-Marne, July 18 – August 6, 1918
- **2** St. Mihiel, September 12–16, 1918
- **3** Meuse-Argonne, September 26 – November 11, 1918

World War II

After significant pressure from African Americans, the War Department began training black pilots and navigators at Tuskegee Army Air Field in 1943. The pilots trained there became internationally known as the "Tuskegee Airmen."

Even the most provincial among African Americans became concerned with the rise of European fascism in the 1930s. In Germany, Hitler and the Nazis rose to power on a platform of racism and anti-Semitism. And African Americans strenuously protested the invasion of Ethiopia, a black kingdom in Northeast Africa, by Italian fascists in 1935. When Hitler's invasion of Poland in 1939 triggered the start of World War II in Europe, the neutral United States was far from ready for war. Blacks were caught in a dilemma: their strong desire to combat Nazism was offset by segregation, discrimination, and oppression at home. "Am I a Negro first and then a policeman or soldier second?" asked the sociologist Horace Cayton. "[S]hould I forget in an emergency situation the fact that . . . my first loyalty is to my race?" The dilemma resolved itself when it became clear that the war provided blacks with an explicit opportunity to link their service to improvements in social justice at home. Black leaders like A. Philip Randolph of the Brotherhood of Sleeping Car Porters embraced a "Double-V Campaign," meaning victory for democracy and racial justice both at home and abroad. He predicted that "before the war ends [blacks will] want to see the stuffing knocked out of white supremacy and of empire over subject peoples."

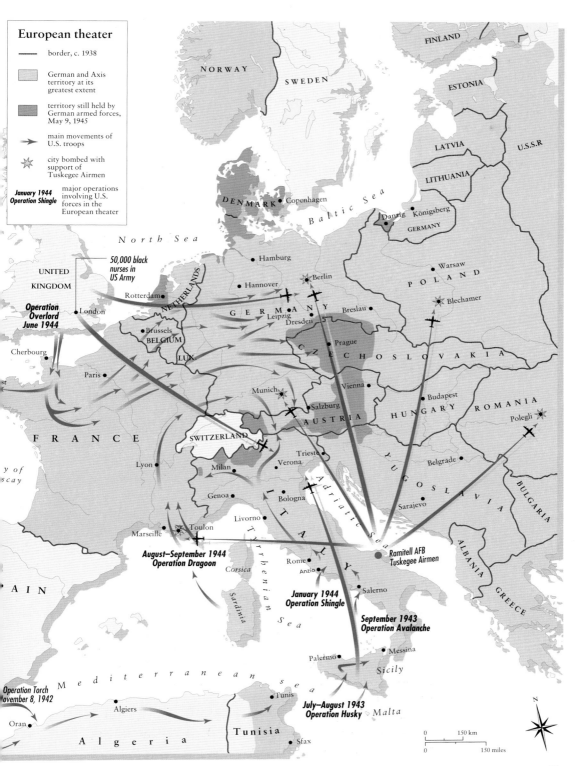

European theater

— border, c. 1938

German and Axis territory at its greatest extent

territory still held by German armed forces, May 9, 1945

→ main movements of U.S. troops

⚹ city bombed with support of Tuskegee Airmen

January 1944 Operation Shingle major operations involving U.S. forces in the European theater

FINLAND

NORWAY

SWEDEN

ESTONIA

LATVIA

U.S.S.R

LITHUANIA

DENMARK • Copenhagen

Baltic Sea

Danzig • Königsberg
GERMANY

North Sea

Hamburg •

50,000 black nurses in US Army

UNITED KINGDOM

Rotterdam • Hannover •

Berlin ⚹

Warsaw •

P O L A N D

Operation Overlord June 1944

London •

NETHERLANDS

G E R M A N Y

Leipzig •
Dresden •

Breslau •

⚹ Blechamer

Cherbourg •

Brussels •
BELGIUM

LUX.

Prague •

C Z E C H O S L O V A K I A

Paris •

Munich ⚹

Vienna •

Budapest •

R O M A N I A

SWITZERLAND

Salzburg •

A U S T R I A

H U N G A R Y

Polegli ⚹

F R A N C E

Trieste •

Verona •

Belgrade •

Lyon •

Milan •

B U L G A R I A

y of scay

Genoa •

Bologna •

Adriatic Sea

I T A L Y

Livorno •

Sarajevo •

Y U G O S L A V I A

Marseille • ⚹ Toulon

Tyrrhenian Sea

Rome •
Anzio •

Ramitell AFB
Tuskegee Airmen

ALBANIA

GREECE

August–September 1944 Operation Dragoon

Corsica

Salerno •

A I N

Sardinia

January 1944 Operation Shingle

September 1943 Operation Avalanche

Mediterranean

Palermo •

Messina •

Sicily

sea

Operation Torch November 8, 1942

Algiers •

Tunis •

July–August 1943 Operation Husky

Malta

N

Oran •

A l g e r i a

Tunisia

Sfax •

0   150 km

0   150 miles

As the United States began gearing up for war, Randolph used threats of a black march on Washington to force the Roosevelt administration to prohibit discrimination in defense industries and government. Black leaders also pressed for impartial administration of the new draft law, and as a result more than 3 million African Americans registered for service in the armed forces under the Selective Service Act of 1940. By the fall of 1944, when the army was at its peak strength, there were 701,678 blacks in that branch of the service alone (there were also 165,000 in the U.S. Navy, 5,000 in the Coast Guard, and 17,000 in the Marine Corps). These approximately 1 million African Americans had a greater opportunity to serve their country than in any previous war.

Black leaders pressed hard to gain for blacks the opportunity to fly in combat. Only with the greatest reluctance and foot-dragging did the Army Air Force agree to train blacks as pilots and navigators, and early in the war veteran black pilots (even those with combat experience in the Spanish Civil War) were rejected out of hand. In 1940, William Hastie, a black federal judge and dean of Howard University's law school, was appointed as civilian aide to the secretary of war to assist with the large numbers of African Americans in the armed forces. Hastie was constantly frustrated in his attempts to fight segregation and secure equal treatment for black soldiers. In a 1943 article, he explained why he resigned in disgust: "Military men agree that a soldier should be made to feel that he is the best man, in the best unit in the best army in the world. When the Air Command shall direct its policies and practices so as to help rather than hinder the development of such a spirit among its Negro soldiers, it will be on the right road."

Partially in response to Hastie's agitation, the War Department began training African Americans as aviation pilots in Tuskegee, Alabama. As in the rest of the armed services during the war, the pilots were segregated from whites—but by the end of the war, the Tuskegee Airmen gained national recognition for their skilled bombing runs from Ramitell Air Force Base in Italy. In July 1943 First Lieutenant Charles B. Hall shot down a German Focke-Wulf FW 190 over the Mediterranean Sea, and became the first African American to score a verified aerial victory since Eugene Jacques Bullard, fighting for France, had downed a German plane during World War I.

Twenty-two black combat units fought in the European Theater. The 761st Tank Battalion helped turn back the Germans in the Battle of the Bulge, and the 614th Tank Destroyer Battalion earned high praise, with one of its officers, Capt. Charles L. Thomas, receiving the Distinguished Service Cross for heroism in action. In the Pacific, the black 24th

Infantry helped take the New Georgia Islands in May 1942. More than 15,000 black troops helped build the Burma Road, which ran from Burma to China and provided Chinese forces with vital supplies needed to defeat the Japanese. And the black 371st Tank Battalion were the first allied troops to liberate the Buchenwald and Dachau concentration camps in 1944.

The World War II experience was a watershed for African Americans. Jim Crow remained intact, but the ideological bases of white supremacy and colonialism were undermined by the horrors of the Holocaust. Millions of blacks, including large numbers of women, were drawn to jobs in defense-related industries. And once again black soldiers used their brave service abroad to press for justice at home.

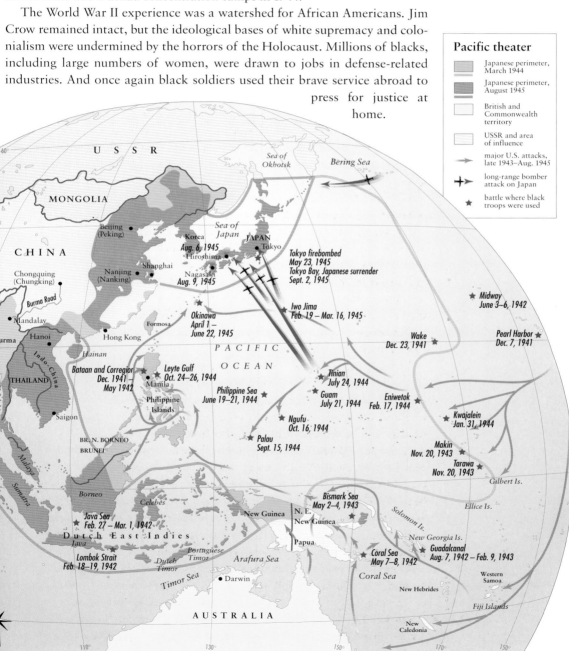

Pacific theater

- Japanese perimeter, March 1944
- Japanese perimeter, August 1945
- British and Commonwealth territory
- USSR and area of influence
- major U.S. attacks, late 1943–Aug. 1945
- long-range bomber attack on Japan
- battle where black troops were used

USSR

MONGOLIA

CHINA

Beijing (Peking)

Chongquing (Chungking)

Nanjing (Nanking)

Shanghai

Korea

Sea of Japan

JAPAN — Tokyo

Aug. 6, 1945
Hiroshima

Nagasaki
Aug. 9, 1945

Tokyo firebombed
May 23, 1945
Tokyo Bay, Japanese surrender
Sept. 2, 1945

Sea of Okhotsk

Bering Sea

Burma Road

Mandalay

Burma

Hanoi

Indo-China

THAILAND

Saigon

Hainan

Formosa

Hong Kong

Okinawa
April 1 –
June 22, 1945

Iwo Jima
Feb. 19 – Mar. 16, 1945

PACIFIC

OCEAN

Wake
Dec. 23, 1941

Midway
June 3–6, 1942

Pearl Harbor
Dec. 7, 1941

Bataan and Corregidor
Dec. 1941 –
May 1942

Leyte Gulf
Oct. 24–26, 1944

Manila

Philippine
Islands

Philippine Sea
June 19–21, 1944

Tinian
July 24, 1944

Guam
July 21, 1944

Eniwetok
Feb. 17, 1944

Kwajalein
Jan. 31, 1944

Ngufu
Oct. 16, 1944

Palau
Sept. 15, 1944

Makin
Nov. 20, 1943

Tarawa
Nov. 20, 1943

Gilbert Is.

BR. N. BORNEO
BRUNEI

Malaya

Sumatra

Borneo

Celebes

Java Sea
Feb. 27 – Mar. 1, 1942

Dutch East Indies

Java

Lombok Strait
Feb. 18–19, 1942

Dutch
Timor

Portuguese
Timor

Arafura Sea

Timor Sea

Darwin

New Guinea

N. E.
New Guinea

Papua

Bismark Sea
May 2–4, 1943

Solomon Is.

Ellice Is.

New Georgia Is.

Guadalcanal
Aug. 7, 1942 – Feb. 9, 1943

Coral Sea
May 7–8, 1942

Coral Sea

New Hebrides

Western
Samoa

Fiji Islands

AUSTRALIA

New
Caledonia

The Cold War: Korea and Vietnam

Although black and white units fought side by side against the Germans in the closing months of World War II, the military's policy was still one of segregation. The long era of segregation in the U.S. Armed Forces came to an immediate end in July 1948 under the express orders of President Harry S Truman. "It is hereby declared," the president ordered, "that there shall be equality of treatment and opportunity for all persons in the armed services without regard to race, color, religion, or national origin." When the president was asked if his advocacy of equal treatment and opportunity in the armed forces foretold the eventual end of segregation in other areas of American society, Truman replied "Yes." He was right: the integration of the military by executive order did presage the end of legal segregation. African Americans took advantage of the executive order to join branches of the military closed to them under segregation, including the Navy, Air Force, and Marines. But blacks still joined the Army in large numbers, even when the battles of the Cold War turned hot. Since 1948, larger percentages of African Americans than whites have served in the armed forces, seeing them as an avenue to better employment and educational opportunities. As a result, black soldiers bore the brunt of the heavy casualties suffered in U.S. involvement in Korea and Vietnam.

When Communist North Korea attacked South Korea in June 1950, one year after Communists triumphed in China, American officials feared all of Asia would follow without an armed response. America's first integrated war, under the flag of the United Nations, began badly: North Korea forced its opponents to retreat to the southeast corner of the Korean peninsula. But in a stunning reversal, U.S. General Douglas MacArthur executed an amphibious landing behind enemy lines at Inchon. With black and white soldiers fighting side by side with startling effectiveness, MacArthur pushed the North Korean troops back to the Chinese border. This was a mistake. Chinese troops entered the war and pushed the U.N. soldiers back across the 1950 border between the two Koreas. With the war at a stalemate, Truman fired MacArthur and initiated peace talks. The armistice line of July 27, 1953, continues to the present day to be one of the most heavily armed places on earth.

There was an even more significant African American involvement in the Vietnam War. As with previous wars, blacks volunteered in large numbers to serve—but even more were conscripted into service by a draft that targeted poor and less educated Americans. Members of the middle and upper classes could more easily evade the draft by entering college or leaving the country, or accept less dangerous assignments in the National Guard. That left many members of the African American community vulnerable to conscription: thirty percent of eligible blacks were drafted, compared to 18 percent of eligible whites. While in Vietnam—which, like Korea, was a war between a Communist North and an anti-Communist South—extremely high numbers of black soldiers were killed and wounded. During 1966–67, for instance, African Americans constituted 11 percent of the total U.S. enlisted personnel in Vietnam; yet black soldiers constituted 22.4 percent of all Army troops killed in action.

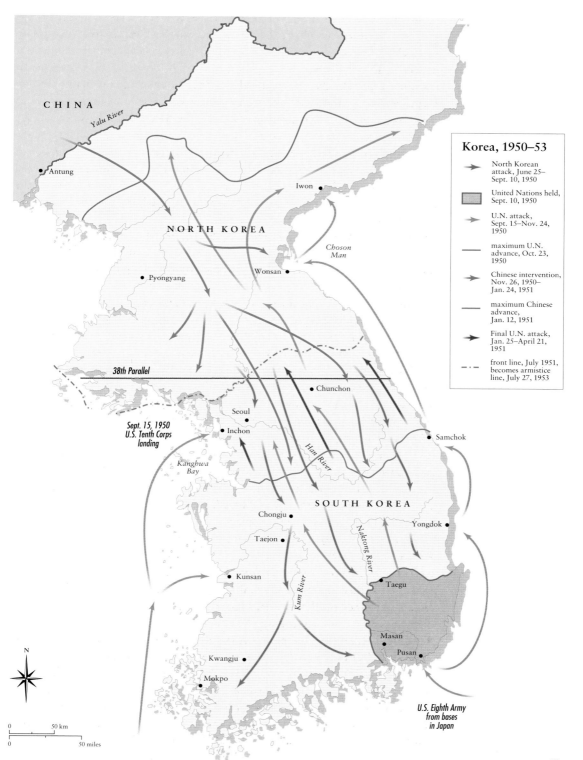

Korea, 1950–53

→ North Korean attack, June 25–Sept. 10, 1950

▨ United Nations held, Sept. 10, 1950

→ U.N. attack, Sept. 15–Nov. 24, 1950

— maximum U.N. advance, Oct. 23, 1950

→ Chinese intervention, Nov. 26, 1950–Jan. 24, 1951

— maximum Chinese advance, Jan. 12, 1951

→ Final U.N. attack, Jan. 25–April 21, 1951

–·– front line, July 1951, becomes armistice line, July 27, 1953

CHINA

Yalu River

Antung

NORTH KOREA

Iwon

Choson Man

Pyongyang

Wonsan

38th Parallel

Sept. 15, 1950 U.S. Tenth Corps landing

Seoul

Inchon

Chunchon

Kanghwa Bay

Han River

Samchok

SOUTH KOREA

Chongju

Yongdok

Taejon

Naktong River

Kunsan

Kum River

Taegu

Masan

Pusan

Kwangju

Mokpo

U.S. Eighth Army from bases in Japan

N

0   50 km

0   50 miles

American involvement in Vietnam began in the late 1950s, but escalated rapidly after an August 1964 incident between American and North Vietnamese ships in the Gulf of Tonkin. President Lyndon B. Johnson used the incident to ratchet up U.S. involvement, ultimately raising the number of U.S. troops to an astonishing 535,000. By 1967 the war was costing the United States more than $2 billion a month and severely threatening Johnson's social programs at home. No matter how much the United States bombed, burned, and razed, the North Vietnamese and their southern allies refused to relent. Then in January 1968 the North Vietnamese surprised the United States with a well-orchestrated campaign called the Tet Offensive. Even though the American military claimed victory, Tet convinced many people in the United States that the conflict was un-winnable. Other ironies stood out as well: at the same time as African American soldiers were bearing more than their share of the war in Vietnam, African Americans at home were confronting economic inequalities and racial tension. Between 1965 and 1969 violent riots swept African American neighborhoods in Los Angeles, Newark, and Detroit. Federal troops were called in to quell the Detroit riot, causing many to see uneasy parallels between action in Vietnam and urban America. In 1968, Martin Luther King Jr. publicly condemned America's role in Vietnam, persuading still more blacks and liberal whites to oppose the war.

Johnson's successor, Richard Nixon, campaigned on a "secret plan" to end the war in Vietnam, yet while in office he widened the bombing of North Vietnam and bombed the neighboring countries of Laos and Cambodia. The latter action caused the largest anti-war demonstrations in American history, yet the United States didn't begin pulling out until early 1973. In the spring of 1975, North Vietnamese armies entered Saigon, and America's longest war ended in ignominious defeat. African American veterans, who faced discrimination while in the armed services only to encounter racism and other difficulties at home, felt this defeat especially keenly.

A soldier from the 173rd U.S. Airborne Division calls for medics to aid a wounded comrade in the Vietnam jungle. Blacks served in Vietnam in numbers out of proportion with their percentage in the general population.

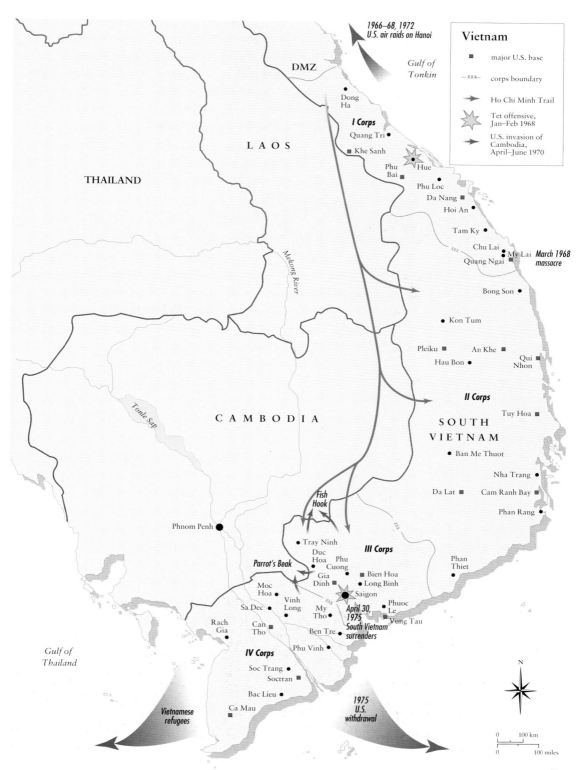

1966–68, 1972
U.S. air raids on Hanoi

Vietnam

- ◼ major U.S. base
- —×××— corps boundary
- → Ho Chi Minh Trail
- ✶ Tet offensive, Jan–Feb 1968
- → U.S. invasion of Cambodia, April–June 1970

Gulf of Tonkin

DMZ

LAOS

THAILAND

Dong Ha

I Corps

Quang Tri
Khe Sanh
Phu Bai
Hue

Phu Loc
Da Nang
Hoi An

Tam Ky

Chu Lai
Quang Ngai
My Lai
March 1968 massacre

Bong Son

Kon Tum

Mekong River

Pleiku
An Khe
Hau Bon
Qui Nhon

II Corps

Tuy Hoa

Tonle Sap

CAMBODIA

SOUTH VIETNAM

Ban Me Thuot

Nha Trang
Da Lat
Cam Ranh Bay

Phan Rang

Fish Hook

Phnom Penh

Tray Ninh
Duc Hoa
Phu Cuong
III Corps
Bien Hoa
Long Binh

Phan Thiet

Parrot's Beak

Moc Hoa
Gia Dinh
Saigon

Sa Dec
Vinh Long
My Tho
Phuoc Le
Vung Tau

April 30, 1975 South Vietnam surrenders

Rach Gia
Can Tho
Ben Tre

Gulf of Thailand

Phu Vinh

IV Corps

Soc Trang
Soctran

Bac Lieu

Ca Mau

Vietnamese refugees

1975 U.S. withdrawal

N

0   100 km
0   100 miles

91

The 1990s: Peacekeeping and the Gulf War

General Colin Powell was the first African American to be named chairman of the Joint Chiefs of Staff, a position he held during the successful war in the Persian Gulf.

The armed forces were especially stung by the "Vietnam syndrome" and tended to resist the use of military force to carry out American objectives abroad. This scenario changed in 1990, when President Bush and Chairman of the Joint Chiefs of Staff General Colin Powell—the first African American to hold the post—sent a massive U.S. force to the Persian Gulf to dislodge Iraqi invaders from Kuwait. Blacks, who made up a little more than 13 percent of the population, accounted for 25 percent of the 500,000 troops sent to the Middle East. Polls taken before Operation Desert Storm began in early 1991 suggested that blacks, dubious of again paying more than their share in a potentially messy war, were less supportive of military action than whites. Yet African Americans expressed ample pride in the strong leadership of General Powell, who emerged as one of the heroes of the Gulf War.

Since the end of the Gulf War, the American military has been involved in several peacekeeping and humanitarian missions, including one in the African nation of Somalia and another in the mostly black Caribbean nation of Haiti. In Somalia, factional infighting left over from the Cold War caused a severe famine in 1991–92. U.S. troops, under the umbrella of a U.N. mission, helped

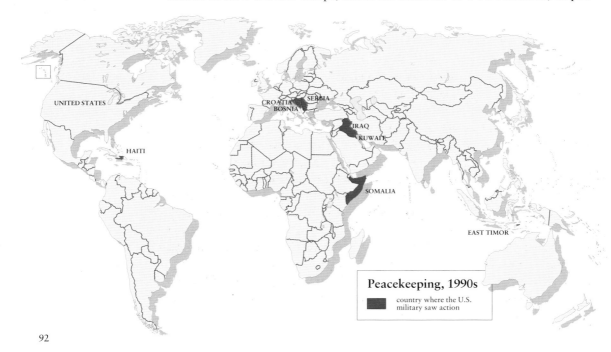

Peacekeeping, 1990s

country where the U.S. military saw action

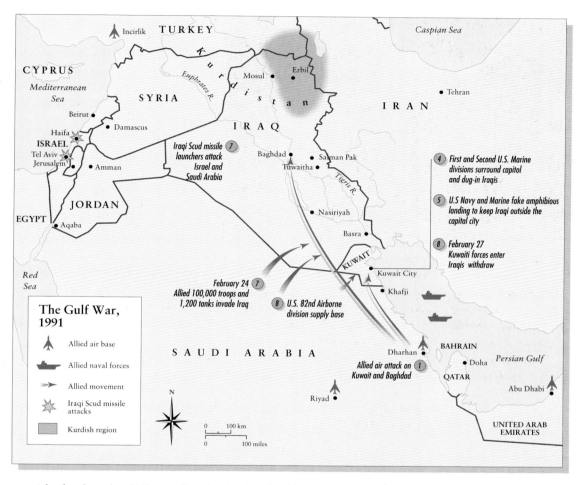

The Gulf War, 1991

Legend:
- Allied air base
- Allied naval forces
- Allied movement
- Iraqi Scud missile attacks
- Kurdish region

Map labels:
- Incirlik
- TURKEY
- Caspian Sea
- CYPRUS
- Mediterranean Sea
- Mosul
- Erbil
- Tehran
- SYRIA
- Euphrates R.
- Kurdistan
- IRAN
- Beirut
- Haifa
- ISRAEL
- Tel Aviv
- Jerusalem
- Damascus
- IRAQ
- Iraqi Scud missile launchers attack Israel and Saudi Arabia (7)
- Baghdad
- Salman Pak
- Tuwaitha
- 4 First and Second U.S. Marine divisions surround capitol and dug-in Iraqis
- Amman
- JORDAN
- Tigris R.
- 5 U.S Navy and Marine fake amphibious landing to keep Iraqi outside the capital city
- EGYPT
- Aqaba
- Nasiriyah
- Basra
- 8 February 27 Kuwaiti forces enter Iraqis withdraw
- Red Sea
- KUWAIT
- Kuwait City
- February 24 (7) Allied 100,000 troops and 1,200 tanks invade Iraq
- 8 U.S. 82nd Airborne division supply base
- Khafji
- SAUDI ARABIA
- Dharhan
- BAHRAIN
- Doha
- Persian Gulf
- QATAR
- Allied air attack on Kuwait and Baghdad (1)
- Abu Dhabi
- N
- Riyad
- UNITED ARAB EMIRATES
- 0 100 km
- 0 100 miles

provide food and relief supplies beginning in May 1992. Caught in the middle of the civil unrest, American soldiers suffered several casualties and public humiliation, leading President Clinton to pull the troops out in the spring of 1994.

American interests seemed clearer with regard to Haiti, with whom relations had been rocky since the island's enslaved residents overthrew their masters in 1794. Haiti's first democratically elected leader, a Catholic priest named Jean-Bertrand Aristide, was ousted by a military junta in October 1991. In September 1994, after persistent pressure by the African American community to reinstate Aristide, 3,000 American troops landed in Haiti and the military agreed to step aside. Six months later, with Aristide back in power, the Americans turned the operation over to U.N. forces. More recently, African Americans in the U.S. armed forces have participated in recent peace-building missions in Bosnia-Herzegovina and Kosovo, where bloody spasms of "ethnic cleansing" in the former Yugoslavia brought them face to face with a people subjected to discrimination and genocide.

PART V: THE STRUGGLE FOR EQUALITY

We know through painful experience that freedom is never voluntarily given by the oppressor; it must be demanded by the oppressed. . . . For years now I have heard the word "wait!" It rings in the ear of every Negro with piercing familiarity. This "Wait" has almost always meant "Never."
—Martin Luther King Jr., 1963

After the Civil War destroyed the Confederacy and slavery, African American families were reunited and blacks used their newly found mobility to move around the country. Southern blacks were given access to the ballot box, and hundreds of black public officials were elected in the 1870s. Ex-slaves founded scores of churches, schools, and mutual-aid societies. But Frederick Douglass, who had labored so long for the end of slavery, was cautious. "The work," he said, "does not end with the abolition of slavery, but only begins." During Reconstruction, when black freedmen, the federal government, and Northerners held sway in the South, it appeared that a true revolution in race relations might be at hand. Yet the substantial victories won by African Americans in both the South and the North were challenged by Southern whites who resorted to violence, terror, and murder.

Southern blacks remained free after Reconstruction ended, but their freedom was stripped away layer by layer. Strict vagrancy laws again limited black mobility. Poll taxes, literacy tests, and physical intimidation kept blacks away from the ballot box. Jim Crow laws separated blacks from whites and brought racial inequality to every corner of life in the South. Lynching and Ku Klux Klan intimidation became the means through which white Southerners enforced a new racial order. According to the black intellectual W. E. B. DuBois, "the slave went free; stood a brief moment in the sun; then moved back again toward slavery."

The period after Reconstruction has been called "the nadir" by one scholar of American race relations, but it was also a period of transformation and construction among the black community. For example, it was during the era of segregation when a lion's share of the nation's black colleges and universities were founded, schools that would educate generations of African American leaders and professionals (and to this day continue to be among the nation's best). Hundreds of thousands of blacks left the

Terrorist organizations like the Ku Klux Klan and the White League threatened the legal rights of newly freed blacks. This Northern political cartoon attacks their methods, which effectively denied African Americans access to education and the ballot box.

rural South for jobs and a brighter future during World War I, an exodus known as the Great Migration. And African Americans founded countless organizations to fight for equal rights and justice in both the North and South. In addition to the well-known National Association for the Advancement of Colored People (NAACP) and National Urban League (NUL), blacks founded groups like the National Negro Business League (NNBL), the National Association of Colored Women (NACW), and the United Negro Improvement Association (UNIA). During the 1920s, African Americans flocked to black neighborhoods like New York's Harlem, where the Jamaican immigrant Marcus Garvey refined the ideology of black nationalism. And even though they were barred from official competition with whites, talented black baseball players like Satchel Paige and Josh Gibson battled it out in the Negro Leagues.

African Americans never stopped fighting for equal rights, even in the darkest days of racial violence in the postwar South. They fought in the courts and legislatures to undermine (and hopefully destroy) unjust Jim Crow laws. They joined groups, unions, and political parties that offered an alternative vision of America. And they commenced numerous mass movements to force society to grant the rights already embedded in the U.S. Constitution. The Legal Defense Fund of the NAACP, for example, waged a relentless battle against segregation laws until the U.S. Supreme Court struck them down as unconstitutional in 1954. One year later, after a seamstress named Rosa Parks refused to give up her bus seat for a white man, blacks in Montgomery, Alabama, unleashed a one-year boycott of the bus system which helped integrate public facilities. One of the leaders of the boycott, Dr. Martin Luther King Jr., engaged millions of blacks and whites in a nonviolent struggle for civil rights.

Under the leadership of King and others, the civil rights movement reached its apogee in the 1950s and '60s. A committed Christian inspired by the philosophies of Mohandas Gandhi and Henry David Thoreau, King used non-violence and direct action to inspire the movement for civil rights, broaden its appeal, and legitimate its strategies and demands. "Give us strength to love our enemies and do good to those who despitefully use us and persecute us," King said in 1956. A new generation joined the movement in the 1960s, inspired by King but impatient with the slow pace of integration. In February 1960 four college students from Greensboro, North Carolina, launched the "sit-in" movement to force the desegregation of facilities like lunch counters, restaurants, and bus stations. The Student Non-Violent Coordinating Committee (SNCC) and the Freedom Riders continued this trajectory, aggressively confronting racist whites adamant about maintaining the racial status quo. The violent reaction of the white South to African Americans' claims helped swing the federal government behind the protesters. At President Johnson's urging, Congress enacted legislation in the 1960s to guarantee civil and voting rights for blacks. One hundred years after the end of the Civil War, African Americans won back the rights gained, and then lost, during Reconstruction.

Lynching and the New Racial Order

Lynchings were a gruesome—and all too common—example of extra-legal violence against African Americans. More than 3,000 blacks were lynched in the South between 1880 and 1930.

After federal troops withdrew from the South in 1877, Southern white supremacists filled the power vacuum with terror, violence, and murder. Paramilitary groups like the Ku Klux Klan, founded to terrorize black Republican voters during Reconstruction, used violence to enforce racist social codes as well. African American pedestrians who refused to "step aside" for whites to pass or black sharecroppers who demanded better terms from white landowners were likely to receive a late-night visit from white-hooded Klansmen. White assaults on African Americans, particularly violence precipitated by lynch mobs, became widespread by the 1880s. These murders, usually to avenge a perceived social or sexual transgression, paralleled the passage of Jim Crow segregation laws.

Lynching was not an exclusively Southern phenomenon, and whites as well as blacks fell victim to mob violence. But between 1880 and 1930, 3,220 blacks and 723 whites were lynched in the South, with the greatest numbers taking place in Louisiana, Mississippi, Alabama, Georgia, and Texas. In the West, which was overwhelmingly white, 38 blacks and 447 whites were victims of lynchings during the same period. The worst year for lynching was 1892, when at least 235 African Americans were killed by raging mobs. By the end of the 19th century, lynching had became almost exclusively racially motivated and mostly confined to the Deep South. Lynchings were frequently preceded by a "trial" in which accusers beat confessions for rape, theft, intransigence, or vagrancy out of a bound victim. Accused blacks were often tortured, burned, stabbed, or shot before being hanged.

Black churches and organizations protested vocally against the killings. In the South, courageous black clergymen and civic leaders confronted lynch mobs, and black newspapers risked almost certain retaliation by publishing anti-lynching articles. A leading crusader against lynching was Ida B. Wells, whose investigative report in the *Memphis Free Speech and Headlight* led racist whites to destroy the paper's headquarters. But Wells could not be silenced: she took her movement for a federal anti-lynching law across the country, arguing that "a national crime requires a national remedy." Wells also sought to disprove the Southern contention that lynch law was necessary to protect white women from black rapists. She found that just one in six lynch mobs even claimed it was avenging the rape of a white woman by an African American man.

Other organizations took up the cause against lynching in the 1930s, including the Association of Southern Women for the Prevention of Lynching. By that time black migration and changes in the regional economy—combined with the successes of the anti-lynching campaigns—had significantly reduced the number of lynchings in the South. In 1953, for the first time, no lynchings were reported in the United States.

Lynchings, by state, 1889–1918

Number of lynchings by state

251 to 386

141 to 250

41 to 140

11 to 40

1 to 10

Proportion of blacks in lynchings, in percent

over 80

51 to 80

under 51

The Spread of Jim Crow

Blacks suffered more than their white counterparts as the Southern economy spiraled downward in the 1890s. Despite this, African Americans became targets for especially virulent white rage during a decade one historian called the "nadir" of the postslavery black experience. Lynchings killed hundreds of blacks per year, and race riots ravaged cities like Atlanta and Wilmington, North Carolina.

Racial discrimination also took on more legal forms. Several state constitutions passed in the South between 1890 and 1900 disfranchised most black voters by using literacy tests, property qualifications, and poll taxes. Whites who were unable to meet the new requirements were often allowed to vote by means of "grandfather clauses." The Supreme Court upheld the disfranchisement clauses in 1898, crippling the Republican Party in the South and handing over state offices to the Democrats for the next 60 years.

In the famous case *Plessy v. Ferguson* (1896), the Supreme Court upheld another kind of law sweeping the South, so-called "Jim Crow" laws. Jim Crow laws (named for a stock character in racist, blackface minstrel shows) mandated regulated racial segregation in public facilities of all kinds, from water fountains to seats on turn-of-the-century streetcars. Homer A. Plessy, a light-skinned black man, was arrested in New Orleans after he refused to ride in a "blacks only" rail car. After a conviction in a Louisiana courtroom, Plessy's case went to the U.S. Supreme Court, which ruled that as long as accommodations for blacks were equal to those of whites, the races could be legally separated. Of course, in the harsh racial realities of the South at the time, facilities were rarely, if ever, equal for blacks and whites. Once blacks were disfranchised and public facilities legally segregated, white supremacy became a reality in the South.

Beginning in Tennessee in 1875, state after state pushed through hundreds of Jim Crow laws, separating blacks and whites on trains, in stations, and on ships. In 1883 (after the Supreme Court declared the 1875 Civil Rights Act unconstitutional) blacks were banned from white schools, theaters, and restaurants. Many African Americans refused to accept the new racial order: in North Carolina, blacks made political alliances with populist whites and initially were able to hold off Jim Crow laws. But in 1898, whites rioted when a black newspaper in Wilmington criticized the tactics of Southern Democrats. The paper's offices were destroyed, as well as several black neighborhoods; North Carolina passed its first Jim Crow law two years later.

Booker T. Washington was the most powerful black leader of the Jim Crow era. In a famous speech in 1895, Washington in effect accepted segregation as a temporary accommodation, in exchange for white support to improve blacks' economic progress, education, and social uplift. In a speech known as the "Atlanta Compromise," Washington told Southern whites, "You can be sure in the future, as in the past, that you and your families will be surrounded by the most patient, faithful, law-abiding, unresentful people that the world has seen. . . . In all things that are purely social we can be as separate as the fingers, yet one as the hand in all things essential to mutual progress." To Washington's African American critics, such sentiments played right into the hands of white supremacists; to his supporters, Washington was playing the best cards in his hand, hoping to gain acceptance through self-reliance and uplift.

African Americans and their white allies formed The National Association for the Advancement of Colored People (NAACP) in 1909 to end forced segregation, provide equal education for blacks and whites, and completely enfranchise African Americans. W.E.B. DuBois was the only African American officer on the original board, and was placed in charge of research and the NAACP's journal *Crisis*. In its pages DuBois clashed with Booker T. Washington's approach to race relations, urging a legal and popular assault on segregation.

The spread of Jim Crows laws in the South

- Northern city where Jim Crow existed in practice before 1896

1875 legal segregation, with date Jim Crow laws passed

segregation practiced but did not pass Jim Crow laws

major race riot at the start of the Jim Crow era, with date

Black Colleges and Universities

Before 1865 blacks had been systematically denied educational opportunities – in fact, teaching slaves or free blacks to read was a violation of the law in many Southern states. As a result, historians estimate that at least 4 million African Americans emerged from slavery illiterate. The ex-slaves, Northern educators, and members of the black clergy combined efforts to set up schools during Reconstruction, most of them in black churches. According to almost every account of the postwar South, freed slaves' hunger for learning was insatiable. This hunger led to the creation of the first colleges and universities for African Americans—institutions that became vital for educating black leaders and their followers during the age of segregation and beyond.

The earliest black colleges—as well as day, night, religious, and industrial schools—were supervised by the Freedmen's Bureau, a federal agency commissioned by Congress in 1865. Cooperating closely with Northern religious and philanthropic organizations, the Freedmen's Bureau helped found more than 4,000 schools for ex-slaves in the South. The teachers at the first black colleges were mostly white Northerners, although the numbers of black schoolteachers grew steadily. By the time the Freedmen's Bureau halted its educational labors, it had spent more than $5 million schooling almost 250,000 African Americans.

Between 1865 and 1877, nearly 50 black colleges were founded across the South with the help of the Freedman's Bureau. Among them were Howard University (named for the Bureau's leader, Union Gen. O. O. Howard), Fisk University, Atlanta University, Hampton Institute, and St. Augistine's College. Howard, located in the nation's capital, has a long tradition of excellence and is especially known for its law school, which trained generations of civil rights lawyers including Charles Johnson and Thurgood Marshall. Booker T. Washington attended Hampton Institute, a vocational school for blacks run by Samuel Chapman Armstrong. At Hampton, Armstrong stressed physical labor and its capacity to promote honesty and fidelity; Washington drank deeply from Armstrong's well and became convinced that to advance, blacks had to perform "useful" work. When Washington assumed leadership of the Tuskegee Institute in Alabama, he made sure the students performed all the chores on campus (including construction, cleaning, and food preparation) as well as provide community services for local whites. Washington's goals were twofold: he hoped to educate Southern blacks in the vocational trades and also convince Southern whites that the education of blacks was in everyone's best interest. Washington's attempts to accommodate white Southerners angered W. E. B. DuBois, who attended Fisk University in Nashville before receiving his doctorate from Harvard. DuBois believed it was vital to train African Americans as scholars and leaders. His impeccable scholarship in the fields of history, sociology, and political science paved the way for other black scholars like E. Franklin Frazier, Carter G. Woodson, Kenneth Clark, and Dorothy Porter.

Before the Supreme Court declared segregated education illegal in 1954, black colleges provided African Americans from the South with their only hope for post-secondary education. The schools suffered from chronic shortages of funds, but provided the backbone for several generations of the African American middle class, educating and training a lion's share of the nation's black doctors, lawyers, businessmen, academics, and other professionals. The schools had a large impact on the black struggle for equality as well: many of the leaders of the civil rights movement were educated in all-black, Southern colleges, including Martin Luther King Jr. (Morehouse College), Ralph Abernathy (Alabama State University), and Jesse Jackson (Agricultural and Technical College of North Carolina). Jackson's alma mater also provided a more direct link to the civil rights movement: students at North Carolina Agricultural and Technical (including Jackson) launched the sit-in movement in 1960, which became the largest direct-action protest in U.S. history. Today, almost 50 years after the Supreme Court struck down forced segregation as "separate and unequal," many of the brightest African Americans choose to attend the nation's excellent black colleges. Schools like Spelman College, Lincoln University, and Bethune-Cookman continue to revitalize and pioneer new trends in American higher education.

Towns with historically black colleges and universities

- college or university

The Great Migration

Southern blacks, mired in a cycle of vicious racism and limited economic opportunities, took advantage of a severe labor shortage during World War I to commence a "Great Migration" to Northern and Midwestern cities. Between 1916 and 1920, some 500,000 African Americans left the rural South for the industrial centers of Chicago, New York, Detroit, Cleveland, Philadelphia, St. Louis, and Kansas City. The Great Migration remade the racial landscape of the entire nation.

Like any mass migration of peoples, the African Americans moving north and west responded to both "push" and "pull" factors. Lynchings, segregation, limited educational opportunities, police brutality, and abuse by Southern whites combined with a series of crop failures to "push" blacks northward. "Pull" factors included well-paid industrial jobs and information, spread by the black press, that Northern cities were havens of opportunity for African Americans. Northern cities were hardly free of racism, but World War I caused a sharp decline in European immigration and a skyrocketing demand for industrial goods. Racially biased factory owners were forced to abandon racist hiring practices, and some even recruited in the Black Belt. African American papers like the *Chicago Defender* expounded on the economic opportunities in the North and printed stories

The Great Migration

→ migration stream

Black population in selected cities, 1920

○ over 100,000

○ 50,000 to 100,000

○ less than 50,000

Changes in black population in cities and Southern states, in percent of increase, 1910–20

+70
+40
+10
0

about successful black immigrants. Copies of the paper were passed from hand to hand in the rural South, and people even sought the paper's help in securing jobs. "There is a storm of our people toward the North and especially to your city," read one letter sent to the *Defender* from a group of black Southern women. "Will you please assist us in securing places as we are anxious to come but want jobs before we leave? We want to do any kind of honest labor. Our chance here is so poor."

The Great Migration practically emptied parts of the Southern countryside. Mississippi, Alabama, Georgia, South Carolina, North Carolina, and Virginia each lost more than 100,000 inhabitants between 1910 and 1920, many of them blacks. At the same time, the size of urban African American communities exploded: Detroit's black population, for example, increased by 611 percent over the course of the decade; Cleveland's and Chicago's grew by 307 percent and 148 percent, respectively. These newcomers had a profound impact on the politics, society, and culture of their new homes.

As with the migration of the Exodusters a generation earlier, entire families or communities often made the trek together. And when people did migrate as individuals, they often did so with the aid of family or friends who had journeyed before them. "I know if you come and rent a big house you can get all the roomers you want," wrote one Chicago migrant to friends in the South. "The people are rushing here by the thousands." Even though the newcomers were often disappointed with the weather, the hard work, or the racial animosity of Northern cities, most of them stayed. Dismayed with the condition of life for most Southern migrants, several New York organizations merged in 1910 to form the National Urban League. The league opened branches in most large cities, and sent members to meet newly arrived migrants to direct them to jobs, housing, and educational opportunities.

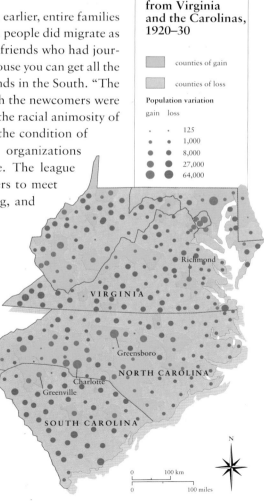

Outmigration from Virginia and the Carolinas, 1920–30

	counties of gain
	counties of loss

Population variation

gain	loss	
.	.	125
•	•	1,000
•	•	8,000
●	●	27,000
●	●	64,000

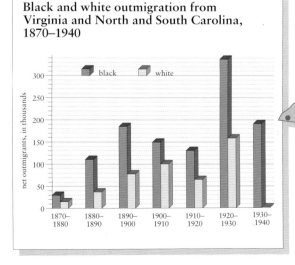

Black and white outmigration from Virginia and North and South Carolina, 1870–1940

Marcus Garvey and the UNIA

The African Americans who migrated North still faced harsh economic realities and vicious white racism. Most migrants could get only low-paying unskilled jobs, and were often crowded into segregated urban slums. Marcus Garvey was the leader who spoke most directly to the hopes, dreams, and disappointments of the urban black population. Garvey urged African Americans to give up on integration (a central goal of groups like the NAACP) and work to create a separate black nation in Africa, complete with an army to protect it. In the meantime, he stressed a program of self-help and racial pride to help American and Caribbean blacks to achieve economic and cultural independence.

Marcus Garvey was born in Jamaica in 1887 and moved to New York City in 1916. His message of black nationalism stressed that blacks were exploited throughout the world and could never count on whites for help. He also preached a brand of racial pride that reverberated strongly in the black community. In the early 1920s, Garvey's United Negro Improvement Association counted millions of members in 38 states and 41 foreign countries. His newspaper, *The Negro World*, reached 200,000 subscribers. UNIA was one of the most successful all-black organizations in history. Many African Americans closely identified with the dark-skinned Garvey, who insisted that "black" stood for strength and beauty, not weakness and inferiority. He led grandiose parades in Harlem wearing a plumed admiral's hat, and his uniformed followers marched in formation.

Although the New York chapter of the UNIA opened restaurants, groceries, factories, and other examples of racial self-sufficiency, Garvey's ultimate vision was of an independent black nation in Africa. "Wake up Ethiopia! Wake up

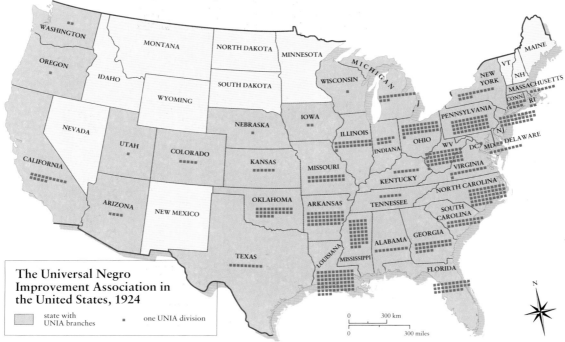

The Universal Negro Improvement Association in the United States, 1924

☐ state with UNIA branches   ▪ one UNIA division

0   300 km
0   300 miles

Africa!" he told his followers. "Let us work toward the one glorious end of a free, redeemed and mighty nation. Let Africa be a bright star among the constellations of nations." Garvey's meteoric success was short-lived, however. He was bitterly attacked by fellow black leaders (W. E. B. DuBois, for example, regarded him as a self-serving demagogue) and the U.S. government. In 1924 Garvey was arrested and charged with mail fraud. He was deported to Jamaica in 1927 after serving one year in prison. Garvey's fantastic rise in the 1920s shows how dubious African Americans were that they would ever be counted as first-class citizens. And his vision of black nationalism endured well beyond his career in the United States.

Marcus Garvey in a black nationalist parade in Harlem. The Jamaica native often appeared in a military-style garb, complete with a plumed admiral's hat and golden epaulets.

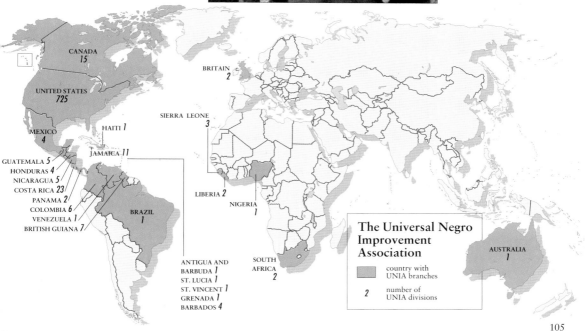

CANADA *15*

UNITED STATES *725*

BRITAIN *2*

MEXICO *4*

HAITI *1*

SIERRA LEONE *3*

JAMAICA *11*

GUATEMALA *5*
HONDURAS *4*
NICARAGUA *5*
COSTA RICA *23*
PANAMA *2*
COLOMBIA *6*
VENEZUELA *1*
BRITISH GUIANA *7*

LIBERIA *2*

NIGERIA *1*

BRAZIL *1*

ANTIGUA AND BARBUDA *1*
ST. LUCIA *1*
ST. VINCENT *1*
GRENADA *1*
BARBADOS *4*

SOUTH AFRICA *2*

AUSTRALIA *1*

The Universal Negro Improvement Association

country with UNIA branches

2 number of UNIA divisions

105

The Negro Baseball Leagues

Baseball, variations of which could be found on American playgrounds for more than a century, soared in popularity in the early 20th century. Before 1900, as baseball became a professional sport, a small number of black players appeared on team rosters. But between 1903 and 1946, players with black skin (whether they were African Americans, Cubans, or Latin Americans) were barred from organized baseball. If black ballplayers wanted to play the sport professionally, they had to create their own all-black teams and play in all-black leagues. As a result, some of the best athletes ever to play the game played for teams like the Monarchs, Black Barons, and Cubans, not the Yankees, Cardinals, and White Sox.

In 1920 Andrew "Rube" Foster organized the Negro National League, with teams in Chicago, Dayton, Detroit, Indianapolis, Kansas City, and St. Louis. In the next decade Cincinnati, Pittsburgh, Cleveland, Brooklyn, Washington, and Philadelphia were added to the league. Even though most of the early players hailed from the South, the cities with teams (with the exceptions of Memphis, Nashville, and Birmingham) were in the North or border states. The teams played in existing ballparks, or rented from white major league clubs, but also played games in Cuba, Puerto Rico, and Mexico, where baseball was not organized along racial lines.

The Negro Leagues were filled with ballplayers of immense talent. Josh Gibson, of the Pittsburgh Crawfords, was known as the "black Babe Ruth," but Ruth could have just as easily been called the "white Josh Gibson." Gibson hit more than 70 home runs in 1931 (records were often sketchy in the NNL) and is believed to have hit more than 1,000 during his career (Babe Ruth hit 715; the current major league record, by ex-Negro Leaguer Hank Aaron, is 755). Leroy "Satchel" Paige, who had one of the most memorable wind-ups in baseball history, claimed to have won 2,000 games in his career. In many ways the Negro Leagues were a great success: teams like the Kansas City Monarchs, a perennial powerhouse in the NNL, were extremely profitable, and large (often integrated) crowds turned up to see the annual East-West all-star game.

It was precisely this success that brought on the NNL's demise. The talent pool among black ballplayers was indisputable, and the size and affluence of black populations in major cities was on the rise. But it took the experience of World War II, where black soldiers helped to defeat racist and genocidal regimes, to fully dramatize the gap between America's democratic ideals and its racist reality. In 1947, Jackie Robinson of the Kansas City Monarchs became a Brooklyn Dodger. His immense talent on the field (he hit .297, led the league in stolen bases, helped the Brooklyn Dodgers win the pennant, and was named Rookie of the Year) and coolness in the face of withering racism made him the ideal man to "break the color barrier" in major league baseball. By 1948, Robinson and the Dodgers had been joined by Roy Campanella, and the

Cleveland Indians had hired Larry Doby and the 42-year-old "rookie" Satchel Paige. It took another ten years before all major league teams had at least one black player. In the early 1950s, an astonishing array of talent gave the major leagues a new crop of black stars: Hank Aaron of the Indianapolis Clowns, Ernie Banks of the Kansas City Monarchs, Willie Mays of the Birmingham Black Barons, and Minnie Minoso of the New York Cubans. The integration of major league baseball spelled doom for the NNL; the league folded completely in 1957. When the black community was given a choice between supporting the Negro Leagues or rooting for major league teams with integrated rosters, they overwhelmingly chose the latter. "When Negro players walked in the big league doors," wrote the *Pittsburgh*

Courier, "Negro baseball walked out." As an unintended result of the integration of major league baseball, many of the greatest players and teams of all time faded, at least temporarily, from memory.

Negro League baseball teams, 1920–50

Rosa Parks and the Montgomery Bus Boycott

After the Supreme Court outlawed segregation in the nation's public schools in 1954, the African American struggle for equal rights entered a decisive new phase: non-violent resistance to Jim Crow laws. Organized protest against segregation was not unknown before 1955, but it was dangerous and forced few changes in either law or custom. Rosa Parks, a seamstress from Montgomery, Alabama, offered blacks there an ideal opportunity to overturn the city's ordinance permitting racial segregation on the city's buses. On December 1, 1955, Parks boarded the 5:30 p.m. bus on Dexter Avenue, exhausted after a long day of work at the Montgomery Fair department store. She walked past the "whites only" seats at the front of the bus and took a seat in one of the back rows that were marked for use by whites or blacks. When a group of white men boarded the bus at the Empire Theater stop and couldn't find seats in the front, the driver issued a command common in the Jim Crow South: "Niggers, move back." Parks, who was 42 and a member of the local chapter of the NAACP, refused. Later, she explained that "the only way to let them know I felt I was being mistreated was to do just what I did—resist the order." The driver got off the bus, summoned the police, and Parks was arrested and taken to jail.

Parks' arrest became the basis for a legal challenge to Montgomery's segregation laws, and later a rallying cry for the revitalized Civil Rights Movement. She was an ideal litigant, and local black leaders took full advantage of the opportunity. Within days, the Women's Political Council of Montgomery mimeographed 52,500 leaflets proposing a one-day boycott of the city's buses. That day, most African Americans walked to work and school, or used a make-shift pool of cars and black-owned taxis. The city's bus company lost between 30,000 and 40,000 fares. In the aftermath of the boycott, the new

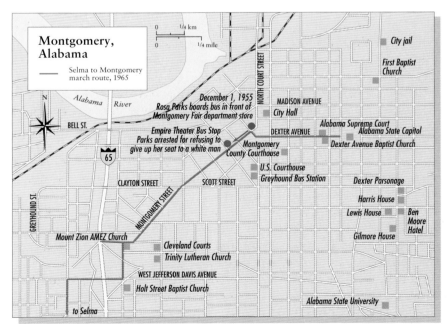

Montgomery Improvement Association elected a new president, Dr. Martin Luther King Jr., the 26-year-old minister of the Dexter Avenue Baptist Church. His first act was to extend the Montgomery Bus Boycott indefinitely. King issued other demands as well: that bus drivers extend courtesy to black passengers; first-come, first-served seating to eliminate the practice of blacks having to give up seats for whites; and the hiring of black bus drivers. When Montgomery's municipal authorities refused to

The Southern Christian Leadership Conference, 1955–65

- Southern state with SCLC activity
- other state with SCLC activity
- city with SCLC activity

even consider the MIA's modest demands, the MIA intensified its wildly successful boycott, which was 99 percent effective. The brunt of the boycott was borne by Montgomery's black women, many of whom worked as domestics and had to walk long distances to work.

Whites in Montgomery tried to harass the African American community into calling off the boycott. Car pools were ticketed by police on trumped-up charges. MIA leaders received threatening phone calls and indictments for violating Alabama's anti-boycott law. And King's house was firebombed on January 30, 1956. But King, a student of the nonviolent teachings of Gandhi and Thoreau, urged the community to remain passive: "We are not advocating violence. We want to love our enemies. Be good to them. Love them and let them know you love them. I want it to be known that . . . if I am stopped, our work will not stop. For what we are doing is right, what we are doing is just." The boycott finally ended on December 21, 1956, after the Supreme Court declared Alabama's bus segregation laws unconstitutional. That day Parks, King, and thousands of other blacks sat at the front of Montgomery's buses.

The boycott graphically illustrated the economic power of the African American community. But the bus victory was a narrow one, and most facilities in Montgomery remained segregated. In fact, Montgomery's white leaders chose to close the city's parks instead of opening them to blacks. The boycott's leaders were vaulted to national prominence. Martin Luther King followed up the victory in Montgomery by joining other black ministers to form the Southern Christian Leadership Conference (SCLC), which aimed to force integration by means of nonviolent civil disobedience. In 1965, King returned to Alabama for his historic march from Selma to the Capitol in Montgomery to register black voters and air grievances about the slow pace of desegregation.

Sit-ins and the Rise of SNCC

On February 1, 1960, four students from North Carolina Agricultural and Technical College in Greensboro launched a radical new phase of the civil rights movement. That day they entered a local Woolworth's dime store, made purchases, then sat down at the lunch counter and ordered coffee. They were refused service because they were black (all seats at the counter were reserved for "whites only"), but they stayed seated until the store closed for the day. The next day they returned with more young people. It was the beginning of the "sit-in" movement, a strategy of peaceful protests against segregation and discrimination, which spread like wildfire across the nation. Young people sat in at white swimming pools, bus stations, hotel lobbies, and restaurants, forcing people to confront the inequalities present in everyday life. "We do not intend to wait placidly for those rights which are legally and morally ours to be meted out to us one at a time," read a newspaper ad purchased by college students in Atlanta.

The demonstrators' courage and moral imperative (and their more aggressive and confrontational tactics) infused new energy into the civil rights movement. Their nonviolent tactics inspired countless others to join the anti-discrimination movement. Soon after the sit-ins began, scores of businesses in the South (including the Woolworth chain's lunch counters) were desegregated, and new, grass-roots organizations began to form. Chief among these were the interracial Congress of Racial Equality (CORE) and the Student Non-Violent Coordinating Committee (SNCC). These new grass-roots activists quickly seized the mantle from the older, more establishment-oriented NAACP and SCLC, and put pressure on the administration of John F. Kennedy to respond to the new demands. It marked a turning point: in 1961 the students forced Kennedy to send federal marshals to the South to protect activists attempting to desegregate buses and waiting rooms; in 1962 and 1963 federal marshals were sent to enforce the integration of several universities in the Deep South.

The SNCC activists prided themselves on their strong ties to local communities. A new generation of African American leaders, including Anne Moody, Julian Bond, John Lewis, Angela Davis, and Stokely Carmichael, emerged from the ranks of SNCC. The protests continued, triggering violent responses from segregationist forces in the South. Civil rights leaders turned to Birmingham, Alabama, in the spring of 1963, calling it the most segregated city in America. Almost nightly, network television broadcast footage of white police officers using dogs and high-pressure water hoses on young blacks protesting segregation in the city. Later that year four African American girls were killed when white supremacists bombed the Sixteenth Street Baptist Church. Thousands took to the streets in nonviolent protest, and when police officers killed two more black children, the timid Kennedy administration was again forced to act.

Angered by the slow pace of civil rights legislation, some of the young SNCC activists began to attack publicly the tactics of established civil rights groups like the SCLC. Long the shock troops of the civil rights movement, SNCC activists felt that established black leaders were not pushing hard enough for full equality. In 1966 SNCC's new chairman, Stokely Carmichael, insisted that blacks use "black power" to combat the "white power" that held them down. Then SNCC embraced the philosophy of Malcolm X to fight back if attacked, and adopted the slogans and rhetoric of nationalists like the Black Panthers. In 1968, the group officially broke with King and the SCLC and agitated for more immediate changes in American society.

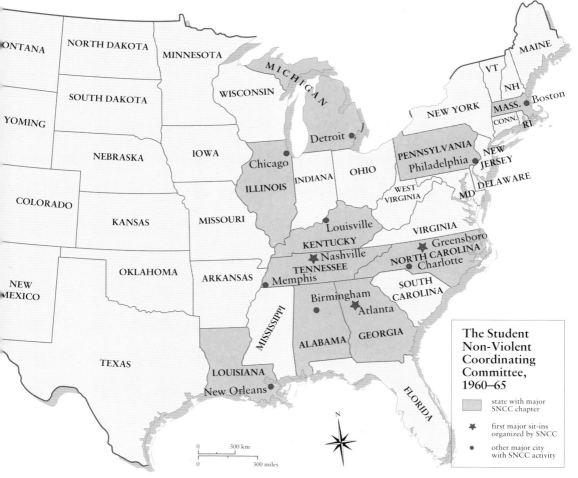

The Student Non-Violent Coordinating Committee, 1960–65

- state with major SNCC chapter
- ★ first major sit-ins organized by SNCC
- ● other major city with SNCC activity

THE ROUTLEDGE ATLAS OF AFRICAN AMERICAN HISTORY

Voting Rights

After the early successes of the sit-in movement, the focus of the civil rights movement shifted from desegregating public facilities to enforcing universal suffrage. The 1964 Civil Rights Act outlawed segregated public facilities and racial discrimination in employment and education, but in many areas of the South, African Americans were still barred from voting. This despite the 15th Amendment, which states that the right to vote shall not be denied on account of "race, color, or previous conditions of servitude." White supremacists utilized a number of tactics to keep Southern blacks disfranchised before 1964, including high poll taxes and literacy tests that kept poor and uneducated African Americans from voting. "Grandfather" clauses enfranchised poor whites. If an African American registered to vote, it usually attracted the attention of the Ku Klux Klan, as well as retribution from employers and local law enforcement.

The Rev. Martin Luther King Jr. participating in a march for voting rights in Montgomery, Alabama, in March 1965. When the peaceful marchers were attacked by mounted state troopers, Congress was forced to act.

When a black voting rights activist named Jimmy Lee Jackson was murdered in Alabama in February 1965, Martin Luther King Jr. and other black leaders organized a march from Selma to the state capitol in Montgomery. On March 7, as the protesters attempted to cross the Edmund Pettus Bridge outside Selma, they were attacked by mounted state troopers. As network television cameras rolled, the police beat, whipped, and tear-gassed unarmed and peaceful demonstrators. Two days later, King decided to retreat as a second march

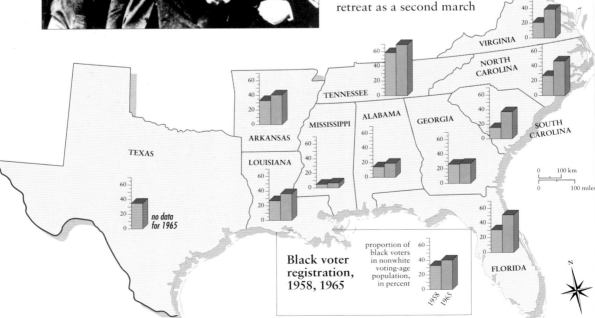

Black voter registration, 1958, 1965

proportion of black voters in nonwhite voting-age population, in percent

was blocked at the bridge. Like his predecessor John F. Kennedy, President Lyndon Johnson was forced to act to aid the demonstrators. On King's third attempt to march to Montgomery, Johnson called the Alabama National Guard into federal service to protect the marchers. More than 50,000 black and white supporters joined the 300 demonstrators as they made their way to the state Capitol.

Johnson had clearly recognized the need for separate federal action to protect the rights of black voters. In an address to Congress and the nation, Johnson quoted the lyrics of a civil rights anthem to make his point: "We intend to fight this battle [for voting rights] where it should be fought—in the courts, in the Congress, and in the hearts of men. And we shall overcome." Within days the president sent Congress his proposals for a voting rights law, and Congress passed it quickly. The Voting Rights Act of 1965 banned literacy tests and other methods to disfranchise blacks, forced suspect counties to obtain Justice Department approval when they changed election procedures, and authorized the attorney general of the United States to send federal examiners to register black voters when he concluded that local registrars were not doing their job.

The Voting Rights Act did not immediately alter voting patterns in the South, but its eventual impact was immense. Federal studies proved that most incidents of disfranchisement occurred in remote rural areas where African Americans made up a majority of the population. In 1967 the attorney general sent federal agents into 62 counties (mostly in rural Alabama, Mississippi, and Louisiana) to register black voters. By 1971, 62 percent of eligible blacks had been registered in the South, compared to 20 percent in 1960. As Colin Palmer, a prominent historian of the African American experience, wrote, "the vote could now be used as a weapon to force other changes upon a reluctant larger society."

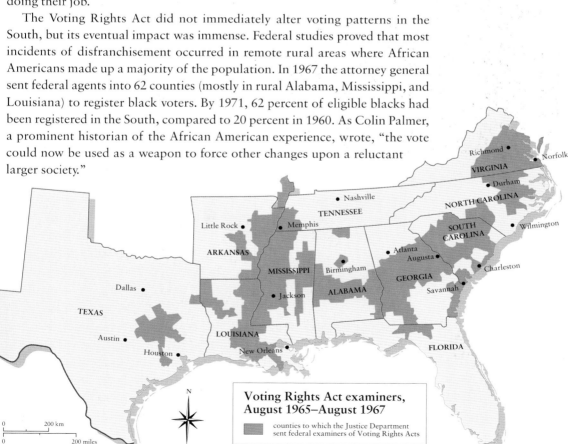

Voting Rights Act examiners, August 1965–August 1967

◼ counties to which the Justice Department sent federal examiners of Voting Rights Acts

African Decolonization and Black Nationalism

At the height of the age of European imperialism, ministers of several countries met in Berlin in the winter of 1884–85 to divvy up the African continent. By the turn of the century, the great powers of Europe had effectively divided Africa for their individual exploitation. The basin of the Congo in Central Africa was "awarded" to King Leopold of Belgium, while England received a huge swath of East Africa stretching from Cairo to Cape Town. France acquired vast portions of North and West Africa including the kingdoms of Algeria, Mali and the Ivory Coast. Germany, Italy, Portugal, and Spain also received colonial possessions.

But the nationalism that led the European countries to become imperial powers also took root on the African continent, especially after World War I. At the insistence of Woodrow Wilson, national identity was used to redraw the boundaries of Europe at the Versailles Peace Conference, and was at the center of the vision for the League of Nations. African people who had been colonial "subjects" for years began to petition and even fight for independence. African Americans, who linked the colonial dependency of Africans with their own subjugation to whites, were central to the movement of decolonization in Africa. Marcus Garvey's Universal Negro Improvement Association transcended national boundaries and helped make "black nationalism" a worldwide ideology. "I do not believe," said the African American scholar W. E. B. DuBois, "that the descendants of Africans are going to be received as American citizens so long as the peoples of Africa are kept by white civilization in semi-slavery, serfdom, and economic exploitation."

The idea that blacks the world over needed to unite to combat racism and colonialism became the basis of a new "Pan-African" movement. DuBois called the first Pan-African Congress in 1919; others convened in 1921, 1923, and 1927. The Ghanian nationalist Kwame Nkrumah recalled how his own movement for independence was inspired by the struggle of African Americans. Nkrumah's movement was among the first in postwar Africa to achieve its goal—it won independence from Great Britain in 1957. Ghana's

Local children play on a toppled statue of the Portuguese founder of Nova Lisboa, in Angola. Angola declared its independence from Portugal in 1975.

success was quickly followed by Nigeria and most of francophone Africa (including Mali, Ivory Coast, Niger, Chad, and Mauritania) in 1960. African Americans were present in large numbers for the ceremonies marking the independence of Kenya, Sierra Leone, and Uganda, and they celebrated when white-run Rhodesia became Zimbabwe in 1980. Andrew Young, an American civil rights leader who became the U.S. ambassador to the United Nations in 1977, said "Africa's emergence from centuries of colonialism made us as African Americans feel part of a world movement for the liberation and self-determination of a subjugated peoples."

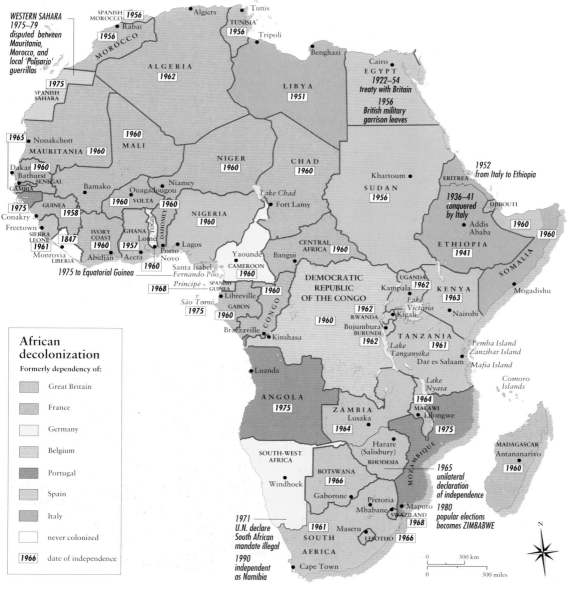

African decolonization

Formerly dependency of:

- Great Britain
- France
- Germany
- Belgium
- Portugal
- Spain
- Italy
- never colonized

1966 date of independence

The Nation of Islam

Blending the methods and arguments of Marcus Garvey with Islamic religion, the Black Muslims became one of the most enduring black nationalist groups in American history. The Hon. Wallace D. Fard founded the Nation of Islam in Detroit in 1929. In its early years, the group grew slowly and won few adherents. The Black Muslims' mission and message changed substantially in 1950, when Elijah Poole, who renamed himself Elijah Muhammad, took control. Muhammad moved the organization to Chicago and opened temples in New York, Detroit, and Los Angeles. Like Garvey, Muhammad preached that blacks should be proud of their African heritage—but he also claimed that whites were devils and inherently evil. This message reverberated powerfully at a time when black nationalism was spreading throughout Africa, creating new black nations, and white segregationists were holding the line in the U.S. South. The Black Muslims rejected all names that implied a connection with slavery and white America and sought economic and physical separation from the white community. This set them dramatically apart from the integrationist strategies of civil rights leaders like Martin Luther King Jr.

Malcolm X emerged in the early 1960s as the chief spokesperson for the Nation of Islam. His fiery pronunciations of black nationalism appealed to large numbers of urban African Americans.

Combining elements of a religious organization, a political party and a social movement, the Nation of Islam spoke to African Americans disgusted with the persistence of racism and second-class citizenship. By far the most eloquent Black Muslim spokesman was Malcolm X. Born Malcolm Little, the Omaha native became a member of the Nation of Islam while in prison. He was named the principle minister of Temple Number Seven in Harlem in 1954. Malcolm X drew large crowds and a tremendous amount of media attention with his bitter denunciations of racism and American society. Whites hated him and integrationist members of the black middle class derided him as an extremist, but he clearly spoke to the needs and desires of dispossessed urban blacks. Like Marcus Garvey, Malcolm X celebrated his blackness. "I am black first," he told one group. "My sympathies are black, my allegiance is black, my whole objectives are black. . . . I am not interested in being an American, because America has never been interested in me." In stark contrast to King's strategies of nonviolence, Malcolm X asserted that blacks needed to resist their condition "by any means necessary." After a pilgrimage to Mecca, Malcolm X moderated some of his views and distanced himself from the Nation of Islam. He was assassinated in early 1965.

Louis Farrakhan, Malcolm X's successor as spokesman for the Nation of Islam, has at the same time marginalized the group and led it toward the mainstream. Farrakhan's separatism and open anti-Semitism (he called Judaism a "gutter religion") has fueled substantial protests against him. He achieved a notable success, however, in October 1995 as leader of the Million Man March in Washington, D.C. To a large crowd (though less than the touted million) of African American men, Farrakhan offered a chance to "atone" for brushes with the law, abusive relationships, or fathering illegitimate children. The protest was peaceful and, for many, inspirational.

The Nation of Islam

● center of importance for the Nation of Islam

• city with mosque(s) by 1997

state with mosque(s)

PART VI: THE AFRICAN AMERICAN COMMUNITY

> We want to be Americans, full-fledged Americans, with all the rights of other American citizens. But is that all? Do we want simply to be Americans? Once in a while through all of us there flashes some clairvoyance, some clear idea, of what America really is. We who are dark can see America in a way that white Americans cannot. And seeing our country thus, are we satisfied with its present goals and ideals?
> —W. E. B. DuBois, October 1926

The black intellectual W.E.B. DuBois wrote these words in the NAACP's influential newspaper *The Crisis* during the heyday of what became known as the "Harlem Renaissance." In the editorial, entitled "Criteria of Negro Art," he wrote of "a new desire to create . . . a new will to be" within the African American community. According to DuBois, this new realization of itself as both quintessentially American and also separate from the dominant, white society, was what allowed the African American artistic community to flourish after World War I. The emergence of African American arts, letters, music, and political activism burst forth on the streets of upper Manhattan in the 1920s and '30s and spread to other locales as well. The black people who made their homes in Northern cities did not find a paradise of racial equality and riches, but they did (along with their kin who remained in the South) make communities that changed the intellectual, political, and cultural life of the nation.

In Harlem, poets like Langston Hughes and Countee Cullen wrote of a black experience that was, at its core, an American experience as well. "I, too, sing America," exclaimed Hughes in one famous poem, echoing (and building upon) the art of Walt Whitman, who took as his muse the masses of New York City a century before. New Yorkers of every color flocked uptown to hear a revolutionary and evolving black musical form called jazz—imported from New Orleans in the second decade of the 20th century—at a nightclub named for the crop African Americans toiled over in slavery and freedom: the Cotton Club. Black orators stood on street corners, extolling the alternative visions of political parties like the Socialists, or the black nationalism of Marcus Garvey's United Negro Improvement Association.

What does the Harlem Renaissance tell us about the African American community in the 20th century? First, that a mostly Southern and rural people was in the process of becoming an urban one. Second, that voices too often repressed and ignored in the South were being heard more loudly than ever before. And finally, that black people had something unique and powerful to say about what it means to be an American. This final part of the atlas does not share the chronological or thematic organization of its predecessors, skipping across the 20th century and mapping snapshots of African American culture, politics, and demographics. The map of Harlem in the 1920s shows how,

A march by the National Association for the Advancement of Colored People (NAACP) to end legalized segregation and racism winds its way through Harlem. The formation of the NAACP in 1909 marked the beginning of the modern civil rights movement.

block by block, an urban neighborhood became a center for the intellectual and cultural life of the United States. Another map shows the diverse geography of black musical contributions, from the Delta blues to hip hop. A third chronicles a profound political shift in the African American community from the Republican to the Democratic Party. Blacks did not abandon the party of Abraham Lincoln to become one of the Democrats' key constituencies overnight, but voting trends underwent a significant change in the 1920s and '30s. Finally, the section concludes with an illustration of black political clout in America's cities and an examination of the African American community as reflected in the 1990 U.S. Census. The picture it portrays is of a community making continual gains and at the same time confronting persistent inequalities and racism. How else to explain the notable increases in black median earnings and educational levels that parallel a poverty and infant mortality rate almost three times that of white Americans? The African American struggle to survive, endure, and prosper in this country continues even as we enter a new millennium.

Since the first Africans arrived on the shores of Jamestown, black people have been a central part of the struggle for freedom in the Americas. It is in this aspect that African Americans' contributions transcend their relatively small numbers and minority status. On one side, in the words of the historian John Hope Franklin, blacks have been "constant reminders of the imperfection of social order and the immorality of its human relationships." On the other, African Americans have used their unique perspective to point out the weaknesses and the strengths, the horrors and the beauty of the American experience.

The Harlem Renaissance

African Americans continued to leave the rural South in unprecedented numbers in the 1920s. And despite the race riots of 1919, most continued to flock to industrial cities in the North. Already established black enclaves in cities like Chicago and New York beckoned to Southern African Americans and even Afro-Caribbeans like Marcus Garvey. Sociologists and demographers began to write about the "black metropolis"—a city within a city containing a complex melange of workers, artists, entertainers, intellectuals, and businesspeople. Nowhere was this mixture more culturally significant than in Harlem, a black neighborhood in upper Manhattan. There black writers, entertainers, and artists created a movement that forever changed the arts in America.

The black historian and writer James Weldon Johnson called Harlem the "Negro capital" of the United States: "[Harlem] is the Mecca for the sightseer, the pleasure-seeker, the curious, the adventurous, the enterprising, the ambitious, and the talented of the entire Negro world." Americans of all races flocked to the Cotton Club on Lenox Avenue to listen to jazz. Authors like Jean Toomer and poets like Countee Cullen helped insert the concept of race into the center of American literature. Harlem also attracted Langston Hughes, who recalled turning down an invitation to see Europe in the 1920s "because I wanted to see Harlem. . . . More than Paris or the Shakespeare country, or Berlin, or the Alps, I wanted to see . . . the greatest Negro city in the world."

Harlem's luxurious brownstones and apartment buildings were built around the turn of the century, before the neighborhood became predominantly African American. Perhaps the most elegant street in Harlem was Edgecombe Street on Sugar Hill, which became the home of elite Harlem society. Nearby was the Dunbar (named for the black poet Paul Lawrence Dunbar), a large garden apartment complex that was home to Harlem luminaries such as the poet Countee Cullen, the intellectual W.E.B. DuBois, the union leader A. Philip Randolph, and the actor/activist Paul Robeson. Langston Hughes settled in southern Harlem, in a brownstone facing Mt. Morris Park, now Marcus Garvey Memorial Park. Other Harlem landmarks include the Apollo Theater, where numerous black entertainers including Ella Fitzgerald began their careers; the Cotton Club, where Duke Ellington's Orchestra was the house band; the 369th Regiment Armory, home of the famed black regiment; and the Abyssinian Baptist Church, home of the largest black Protestant congregation in the United States.

The Harlem Renaissance displayed significant longevity, stretching into the darkest days of the Great Depression. Zora Neale Hurston, a brilliant intellectual and anthropologist, began collecting American and Caribbean folklore in the late 1920s. She wrote short stories, scholarly articles, and novels including *Moses, Man of the Mountain, Their Eyes Were Watching God*, and *Dust Tracks on the Road* between 1931 and 1943. The confidence and creativity of the Harlem Renaissance helped to rejuvenate entire ranges of American art in the 20th century. It also provided inspiration for generations of black and white artists, writers, and activists to come.

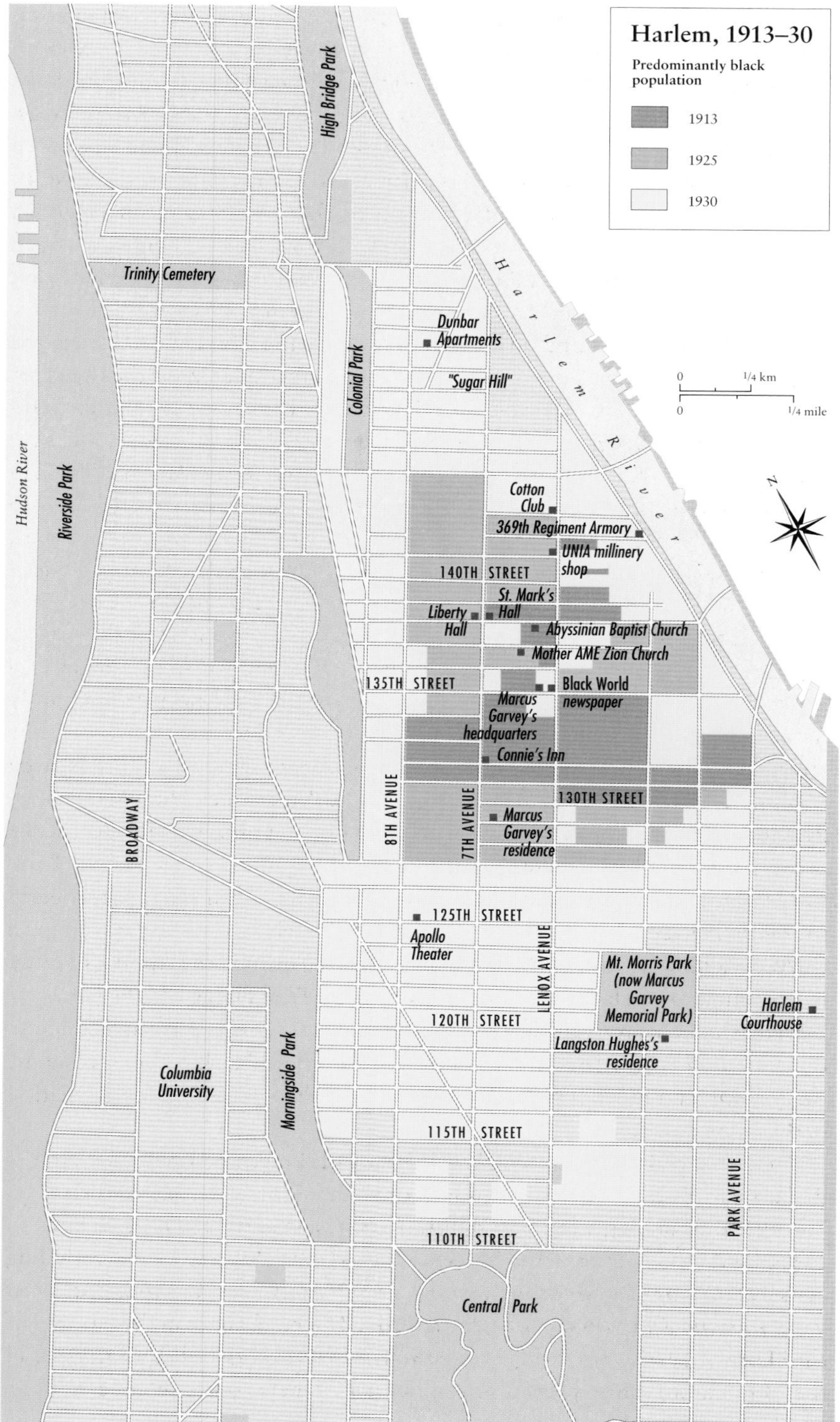
Harlem, 1913–30
Predominantly black population
1913
1925
1930
0 1/4 km
0 1/4 mile
N
Hudson River
Riverside Park
High Bridge Park
Trinity Cemetery
Colonial Park
Harlem River
Dunbar Apartments
"Sugar Hill"
Cotton Club
369th Regiment Armory
UNIA millinery shop
140TH STREET
St. Mark's Hall
Liberty Hall
Abyssinian Baptist Church
Mother AME Zion Church
135TH STREET
Black World newspaper
Marcus Garvey's headquarters
Connie's Inn
130TH STREET
Marcus Garvey's residence
8TH AVENUE
7TH AVENUE
BROADWAY
125TH STREET
Apollo Theater
LENOX AVENUE
Mt. Morris Park (now Marcus Garvey Memorial Park)
Harlem Courthouse
120TH STREET
Langston Hughes's residence
Columbia University
Morningside Park
115TH STREET
PARK AVENUE
110TH STREET
Central Park

African American Musical Traditions

African Americans and whites flocked to the Cotton Club in Harlem to hear jazz music. The nightclub—home to Duke Ellington's band— epitomized uptown elegance during the Harlem Renaissance.

The African American musical tradition stretches back to songs and laments brought from Africa on the Middle Passage. Work songs, "shouts," and spirituals were always part of the lives of African Americans. In the 20th century, black Americans fashioned entirely new and significant musical traditions onto the older genres, including jazz, blues, and rock 'n' roll. With the advent of new technologies like radio and sound recording, African American music spread across the globe.

In the early 1900s, blacks from the Mississippi Delta and various other regions in the South developed a distinctive musical style called the blues. Ragtime, a distinctive new musical form that composers like Scott Joplin fashioned out of classically European and American techniques, was popular at the same time. The streets, clubs, bars, and brothels of New Orleans became a breeding ground for a new, American art form called jazz, which incorporated influences from both the blues and ragtime. Black and white audiences found the new sound irresistible. Jazz followed the Great Migration to places like Kansas City, Chicago, and New York, where the music's spontaneity, its overt sexuality ("jazz" was well-known as a slang term for sex), and its contagious rhythms and melodies packed cabarets and nightclubs during what became known as the "Jazz Age." Many early jazz greats, including Louis Armstrong, Bessie Smith, and Jelly Roll Morton influenced the next generation of performers to expand the music into a new, modern art form. Duke Ellington emerged in the 1920s as one of the greatest composers of all time, perfectly encapsulating jazz music's innovative creativity.

WASHINGTON

OREGON

IDAHO

NEVADA

UTAH

CALIFORNIA

Los Angeles
Charlie Mingus

ARIZONA

The blues also survived on its own, and artists like Ma Rainey, Robert Johnson, and Tampa Red (Hudson Woodbridge) each made contributions to the music's unique communication of loneliness and longing. Jazz underwent significant transformations in the 1930s, with "swing," and the 1940s, when Charlie Parker, Dizzy Gillespie, and Thelonious Monk helped invent "bebop." In the 1950s, rock 'n' roll burst on the scene as an amalgam of blues and country traditions. Little Richard and James Brown inspired both blacks and whites, and Ray Charles helped fashion a new genre called soul. Soul eventually became associated with Detroit, where the black-owned "Motown" label recorded blockbuster artists including the Supremes, Smokey Robinson, and the Jackson 5. In the late 1970s, young African American disc jockeys from poor urban neighborhoods combined elements of funk, disco and rock with older black, oral traditions to create rap. Rap's anti-establishment lyrics (often directed against white police officers) angered many politicians but became wildly popular with young people of all races. It is only the latest example of the African American musical tradition and its continued ability to affect global popular culture.

African American music

- Jazz epicenter
- → Jazz spread
- *Charles* Jazz musician
- Blues epicenter
- *Smith* Blues musician
- Bop epicenter
- *Monk* Bop musician
- Soul/Motown epicenter
- *Wonder* Soul/Motown musician
- Hip Hop epicenter

African American Culture

African Americans' cultural heritage is both diverse and complex, drawing from a deep well of influences including West Africa, the Caribbean, the American South, and the urban environment. Perhaps this is why, as scholars like Henry Louis Gates Jr. have argued, blacks have had such a dramatic effect on the wider culture of the United States as a whole. On the one hand separate and different, African Americans have repeatedly (and profoundly) used their uniqueness to speak to human conditions and emotions that are shared by everyone. As an example, Gates cites the way the African American author Toni Morrison (who won the Nobel Prize for Literature in 1993) takes "the blackness of the culture for granted, as a springboard" to write about the larger American and, indeed, human, experience.

Morrison has used her home state of Ohio, which shares a border with the former slave state of Kentucky, as a setting for her fiction, most memorably in *Beloved*, a ghost story about life after slavery. Many significant black authors have come from Southern states, including Zora Neale Hurston and James Weldon Johnson (Florida), Richard Wright (Mississippi), and Alice Walker (Georgia). Ralph Ellison (Oklahoma), Gwendolyn Brooks (Kansas), and Lorraine Hansberry (Illinois), all of whom deal honestly and dramatically with the topic of race in their fiction, hail from the Midwest. The "black Mecca" of Harlem produced many significant black authors, including James Baldwin, Toni Cade Bambara, and Paul Marshall.

African American contributions to American music, from gospel to jazz to rock 'n' roll, cannot be overstated. Duke Ellington, perhaps America's greatest composer, was born in Washington, D.C., in 1899. Jazz great and bebop legend

Charlie Parker, and jazz and rythm 'n' blues singer Big Joe Turner both came from post-Great Migration Kansas City, Missouri. Paul Robeson, a multitalented actor, athlete, orator, and baritone, came from a small but well-established black community in Princeton, New Jersey. The Mississippi Delta region produced Bluesmen B. B. King (Indianola), Muddy Waters (Rolling Fork), Mississippi John Hurt (Teoc), and Robert Johnson (Hazelhurst). Other blues singers hailed from a wide swath across the South, ranging from Chattanooga, Tennessee (Bessie Smith), Columbus, Georgia (Ma Rainey), Albany, Georgia (Ray Charles), and tiny Shiloh, Louisiana (Leadbelly). African Americans have also made substantial contributions to American culture in the visual arts (painter Jacob Lawrence and photographer Gordon Parks), dance (choreographer Alvin Ailey), and film (Melvin Van Peebles and Spike Lee).

African American artists

author
musician
painter
dancer

Black Political Realignment, 1928–40

Between the Civil War and the election of 1928, an overwhelming majority of African American voters were Republicans. This loyalty was completely understandable: from its inception in 1854, the Republican Party was anti-slavery. The Democratic Party, on the other hand, was closely identified with slaveholders and secession. The first Republican President, Abraham Lincoln, had signed the Emancipation Proclamation, and his allies and successors passed and (for a time) enforced the 13th, 14th, and 15th amendments. During Reconstruction, newly enfranchised black voters in the South helped the Republican Party achieve national political hegemony that lasted until at least 1880.

The South remained overwhelmingly Democratic after Reconstruction, and the party solidified its dominance by disfranchising African Americans and passing Jim Crow laws. When they could, blacks voted against Southern racism and the Democratic Party by voting Republican, which they did in every major local, state, and national election for more than 60 years. Not that a single 20th-century Republican president had even remotely approached Lincoln's legacy. At first Theodore Roosevelt, who publicly opposed lynching, appointed blacks to federal offices, and sought the advice of Booker T. Washington, seemed likely to fill Lincoln's shoes. But Roosevelt retreated significantly in his second term, and African American voters began to feel abandoned by the "party of Lincoln."

By the late 1920s, the national Republican Party hit upon a new strategy: to use its conservative principles to woo white Southern voters. This "lily-white" strategy, combined with the economic misery of the Great Depression, began a process by which African American voters switched their party allegiances. In 1934, Arthur W. Mitchell switched from Republican to Democrat and won election to the House of Representatives from Illinois. Mitchell was the first black Democrat elected to Congress. New Deal Democrats in Northern cities—and especially in New York and Chicago—began reaching out to black voters and promising relief from the Great Depression. Like most other Americans, black voters supported the policies of Democratic President Franklin Delano Roosevelt.

African Americans especially responded to Roosevelt's "Black Cabinet," an unofficial group of prominent blacks who advised the president on race relations, and to the first lady Eleanor Roosevelt, who publicly associated with blacks and was an outspoken proponent of racial equality. Many older blacks continued to vote Republican, but in New York City more than 81 percent of black voters cast Democratic ballots in 1936—an increase of almost 50 percent from 1928. New Deal programs like the Works Progress Administration (WPA) and the National Recovery Administration (NRA) helped African Americans learn to read and get back on their feet financially. The WPA also sent oral historians to interview aging ex-slaves about their lives before and during the Civil War.

Southern blacks were less likely to support the party of Roosevelt, because to them, the Democratic Party was and had always been the party of segregation and white supremacy. Today, however, a large majority of both Northern and Southern blacks routinely cast votes for Democratic candidates while, in another major political shift, many of the former "Dixiecrats" have become Republicans.

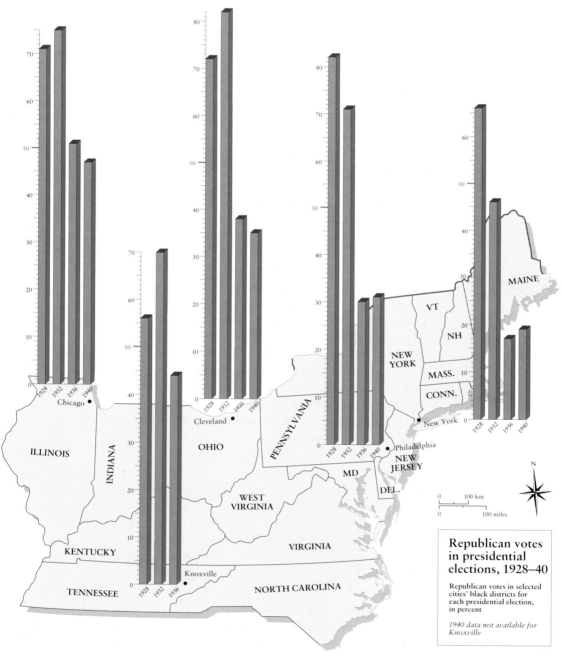

Republican votes in presidential elections, 1928–40

Republican votes in selected cities' black districts for each presidential election, in percent

1940 data not available for Knoxville

Urbanization and Black Mayors

After World War II, blacks continued to leave the rural South in large numbers, with a large majority moving to cities in the North and West. Such cities as Chicago, Cleveland, New York, Detroit, and Philadelphia experienced explosions in black residents. But blacks moved to Southern cities, too. New Orleans, Atlanta, Charleston, Montgomery, Birmingham, and Baltimore each received huge influxes of African Americans in the postwar years. Increasingly concentrated in cities, in black neighborhoods called ghettos, African Americans contributed a growing share of the electorate in states like New York, Illinois, Ohio, Pennsylvania, and Michigan. No longer could politicians for local and national office ignore the black population at election time. Although black voters formed a small proportion of the electorate as a whole and often faced intimidation, harassment, and even violence at the polls, they often had an impact on the electoral outcome in several cities. In some localities, blacks banded together to enhance their political clout. The Atlanta Negro Voters League, for example, conscientiously represented the black constituency for decades. By 1954, blacks had been elected to office in 11 municipalities in the South.

Mass migration to urban areas and this growing awareness of the power of the ballot box propelled hundreds of African Americans into elective office after 1954, especially at the citywide level. The first black mayor was elected in 1885 with the incorporation of Princeville, North Carolina, the oldest black incorporated town in the country. Since then hundreds of blacks have been elected mayors in the United States, in majority-black and majority-white towns alike. Between 1963 and 1973 blacks served as mayors of large cities such as Los Angeles, Newark, Cleveland, and Gary, Indiana, as well as dozens of small towns including Tuskegee, Alabama, and Fayette, Arkansas. The decade of the 1970s saw the elections of African American mayors to large Southern cities like New Orleans and Atlanta. In the 1980s, African Americans won mayoral races in other significant cities: Harold Washington in Chicago, Sharon Pratt Kelley in Washington, D.C., and David Dinkins in New York.

By 1990, 314 African Americans were mayors of their cities, nearly twice the number in 1980 and eight times as many as in 1970. In the 1990s African American mayors of the nation's largest cities either stepped down or were defeated for re-election. But in 1999, there were black mayors in cities and towns as varied as Houston, Texas (Lee Brown); San Francisco (Willie Brown); Pasadena, California (Chris Adams); Trenton, New Jersey (Douglas Bradley); Detroit, Michigan (Dennis Archer), and Minneapolis, Minnesota (Sharon Campbell).

Black elected officials, 1970–90

	members of Congress	state senators	state representatives	county officials	mayors	city council members	school board members	total black elected officials	percentage of change
1970	10	31	137	92	48	552	362	1,469	-
1975	18	53	223	305	135	1,237	894	3,503	138.5
1980	17	70	247	451	182	1,809	1,149	4,912	40.2
1985	20	90	302	611	286	2,189	1,368	6,056	23.3
1990	26	108	340	810	314	2,972	1,561	6,131	1.2

Cities with black mayor, 1999

City size, in inhabitants

- over 1 million
- 500,000 to 1 million
- 100,000 to 500,000
- 50,000 to 100,000

0   300 km

0   300 miles

African American Population, 1990

According to the 1990 U.S. Census, there were 29,986,000 African Americans in the United States. Blacks thus made up 12 percent of the total population of 248,710,000.

The historical legacy of slavery continues to affect where African Americans live at the end of the 20th century. The states with the highest percentages of African Americans are all former slaveholding states: Mississippi (35%), South Carolina (30%), Louisiana (29%), Georgia (27%), Alabama (26%), Maryland (23%), and North Carolina (22%). Yet the Great Migration of the 20th century has also placed an indelible African American mark on the country's urban landscape. The largest populations of African Americans are in New York (2.1 million), Chicago (1.4 million), Detroit (800,000), Philadelphia (700,000), and Los Angeles (600,000). Large cities (those with a population of 300,000 or higher) with the greatest percentages of blacks are still mostly in the South: Washington, D.C (70%), Atlanta (67%), New Orleans, (55%) and Memphis (40%), with the exception of Detroit (65%).

Although African Americans have made tremendous strides in the struggle for equality in the United States, demographic evidence suggests blacks still lag behind in significant areas. Income is one: nowhere in the United States is the median African American family income ($18,098) equal to that of the white family ($30,853). The greatest disparities exist in the Midwest and Northeast. Twenty-nine percent of black families live below the poverty line while only 11 percent of white families do. The rate of infant mortality for African Americans is more than twice as high as for whites, and blacks attain 11.5 years of education compared to 12.5 years for whites. Despite the centuries-old struggle for America to live up to the words in the Declaration of Independence—that all men are created equal and endowed by their creator with the inalienable rights of life, liberty, and the pursuit of happiness—it is clear that true equality, be it racial, economic, or gender-based, has proved an elusive goal.

A multicultural crowd gathers on the streets of Brooklyn, New York for a recent West India Day parade, highlighting the diversity of the cities black population.

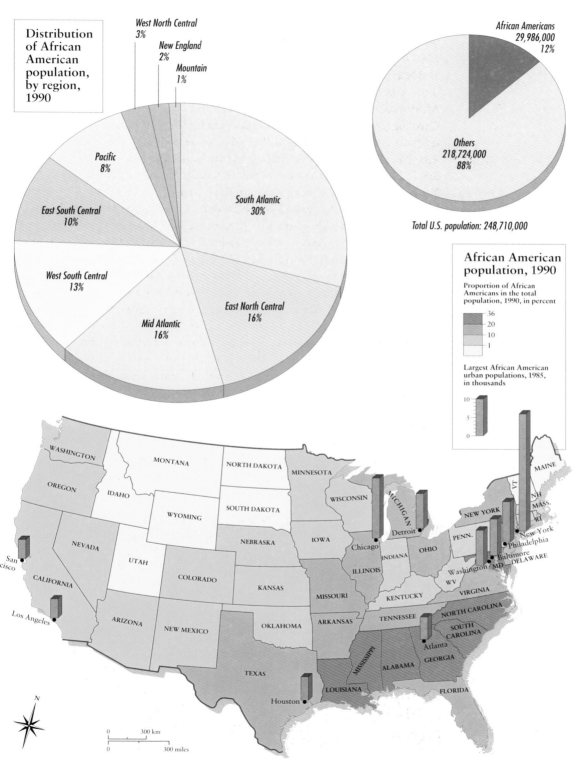

Distribution of African American population, by region, 1990

West North Central 3%

New England 2%

Mountain 1%

Pacific 8%

East South Central 10%

South Atlantic 30%

West South Central 13%

Mid Atlantic 16%

East North Central 16%

African Americans 29,986,000 12%

Others 218,724,000 88%

Total U.S. population: 248,710,000

African American population, 1990

Proportion of African Americans in the total population, 1990, in percent

36
20
10
1

Largest African American urban populations, 1985, in thousands

10
5
0

131

Chronology

3200 B.C.	Egypt founded in Nile River Valley in Northeast Africa.
A.D. 610–733	Islamic faith spreads across Northern Africa.
700–900	North African Berbers establish Trans-Saharan slave trade.
900–1200	Ghanaian Empire reaches its peak.
1200–1450	Empire of Mali reaches its peak.
1450–1800	Songhay Empire reaches its peak.
1494	Treaty of Tordesillas divides New World between Portugal and Spain.
1502	Portuguese ships begin transporting West African slaves to New World.
1619	Dutch merchant delivers 20 Africans to Jamestown colony in Virginia.
1641	Massachusetts becomes first British North American colony to legalize slavery.
1661	Maryland mandates slavery as a life-long condition for Africans and their children.
1739	Stono Rebellion near Charleston, South Carolina; 80 slaves and 20 whites killed.
1741	Great Negro Plot detected in New York City.
1770	Crispus Attucks killed by British soldiers in Boston Massacre.
1770	Phillis Wheatley publishes her first poem, "On the Death of the Reverend George Whitefield."
1775	British General Lord Dunmore offers to free slaves willing to join British Army.
1775–83	More than 5,000 free blacks serve in Continental Army; at least that many runaway slaves and free blacks fight with the British.
1775	First abolition society organized by Philadelphia Quakers.
1776	33 enslaved Africans die in a revolt at Cape Coast Castle slave fort.
1777	Vermont bans slavery in Constitution; first state to do so.
1780	Massachusetts judge rules that state's bill of rights outlaws slavery.
1787	Northwest Ordinance bans slavery in territory north and west of the Ohio River.
1787	Slavery written into U.S. Constitution.
1789	Olaudah Equiano publishes *The Interesting Narrative of Olaudah Equiano*.
1790	The Rev. Richard Allen founds the African Methodist Episcopal (A.M.E.) Church in Philadelphia.
1791	Haitian Revolution begins with a slave revolt.
1791	Astronomer Benjamin Banneker issues the first edition of his almanac.
1793	Congress enacts the first Fugitive Slave Law, requiring free states to return runaways.
1793	Inventor Eli Whitney builds cotton gin; makes cotton a profitable crop and reinvigorates slavery.
1794	Toussaint L'Ouverture overthrows French rule in Haiti, proclaims a republic.
1800	Virginia militia thwarts Gabriel Prosser's slave conspiracy.

1808	Foreign slave trade officially ended by U.S. Constitution.
1820	Missouri Compromise establishes 36°30' parallel as dividing line between slave and free states.
1821	New York erects $250 property qualification for black voters at the same time it eliminates such requirements for whites.
1822	Denmark Vesey slave conspiracy foiled in Charleston, S.C.
1827	John Russworm and Samuel Cornish publish first edition of *Freedom's Journal* in New York.
1829	David Walker's radical *Appeal . . . to the Colored Citizens of the World* widely circulated along eastern seaboard.
1831	Abolitionist William Lloyd Garrison publishes first issue of the *Liberator*.
1831	Nat Turner leads bloodiest slave revolt in U.S. history in Southampton County, Virginia, killing 55 whites; Turner and at least that many killed in retaliation.
1838	Frederick Douglass escapes from slavery and begins career as an abolitionist writer and lecturer.
1841	Upstate New Yorker Solomon Northrup kidnapped and sold into slavery.
1846	"Wilmot Proviso" attempts to ban slavery in territory acquired as a result of Mexican War.
1848	Ellen Craft poses as a sick slaveholder as she and her husband escape from slavery. Anti-slavery Free Soil Party founded.
1850	Compromise of 1850 admits California as a free state, bans the slave trade in Washington, D.C., and enacts a strict Fugitive Slave Law.
1853	Kidnap victim Solomon Northrup rejoins his family in New York.
1854	Kansas-Nebraska Act opens vast new territory to slavery and leads to formation of anti-slavery Republican Party.
1854	Fugitive slave Anthony Burns returned to slavery as thousands in Boston line the streets in protest.
1857	In Dred Scott Decision, U.S. Supreme Court declares slaves are not citizens and rules Missouri Compromise unconstitutional.
1859	John Brown leads raid on federal arsenal at Harper's Ferry in Virginia.
1861	Southern states form Confederate States of America. Civil War begins.
1862	Congress passes Contraband Act, classifying runaway slaves as contraband of war.
1863	Lincoln issues Emancipation Proclamation, declaring slaves in rebellious states to be "forever free." Union Army's ban on black soldiers lifted; 186,000 African Americans enlist during final two years of the Civil War. Black soldiers of the 54th Massachusetts fight bravely in assault on Ft. Wagner.
1865	Lincoln assassinated. Southern states enact "Black Codes." Congress passes 13th Amendment forever outlawing slavery. Reconstruction begins.

1866	Congress passes 14th Amendment granting citizenship to African Americans. Ku Klux Klan formed in Tennessee. Congress authorizes establishment of four permanent black units to fight Indians in the West. Fisk University founded as Fisk Free Colored School in Nashville.
1869	Congress passes 15th Amendment enfranchising black men.
1870–71	Federal Ku Klux Klan Acts attempt to protect black voters from white terror.
1875	Tennessee becomes first state to institute Jim Crow law.
1877	Federal troops withdraw from the South; Reconstruction ends.
1880	60,000 "Exodusters" leave Nashville for Kansas.
1880s	Southern states institute Jim Crow laws.
1884	European nations convene in Berlin and divide Africa into colonies.
1890	Mississippi begins using literacy tests to disfranchise black voters.
1892	A record 235 African Americans killed by lynch mobs.
1896	In *Plessy v. Ferguson*, U.S. Supreme Court upholds Jim Crow laws as constitutional.
1909	African Americans and their white allies form the National Association for the Advancement of Colored People (NAACP) to end forced segregation.
1910	Several organizations merge to form the National Urban League (NUL) to direct black immigrants to jobs, housing, and educational opportunities.
1912	Self-proclaimed "inventor of jazz," Ferdinand "Jelly Roll" Morton, publishes his first song, "The Jelly Roll Blues."
1916	Great Migration begins; 500,000 leave rural South by 1920.
1917	Jamaican immigrant Marcus Garvey founds the Universal Negro Improvement Association (UNIA).
1917–19	More than 400,000 African Americans serve in U.S. Army during World War I.
1917	James Weldon Johnson publishes *Fifty Years and Other Poems*; marks beginning of the Harlem Renaissance.
1919	W.E.B. DuBois convenes first Pan-African Congress.
1920	Negro National Baseball League founded.
1926	Langston Hughes, the poet laureate of the Harlem Renaissance, publishes *Weary Blues*.
1929	Nation of Islam (Black Muslims) formed in Detroit.
1932	African Americans begin to switch allegiance from the Republican to the Democratic Party.
1937	Zora Neale Hurston publishes *Their Eyes Were Watching God*.
1940	The War Department begins training black pilots at Tuskegee, Alabama.
1944	U.S. Army reaches peak strength during World War II; 701,678 African Americans in service in U.S. Army.
1945–47	Jazz greats Thelonious Monk, Charlie Parker, and Dizzy Gillespie pioneer "bebop" jazz at Minton's Play House, an after-hours club in Harlem.

1947 Jackie Robinson joins the Brooklyn Dodgers, breaking the color barrier in major league baseball.

1948 President Harry S Truman integrates the U.S. armed forces.

1954 U.S. Supreme Court declares segregation unconstitutional in *Brown v. Board of Education of Topeka, Kansas.*

1955 Montgomery bus boycott begins when Rosa Parks refuses to give up her seat to a white man. The one-year boycott brings Dr. Martin Luther King Jr. to national prominence.

1957 President Eisenhower sends troops to enforce school desegregation in Little Rock, Arkansas. Southern Christian Leadership Conference (SCLC) formed. Several African Americans on hand as Ghana wins independence from Great Britain.

1959 Berry Gordy founds Motown Records in Detroit.

1960 Four students from North Carolina A&T College launch the sit-in movement at the Greensboro, N.C., Woolworth's lunch counter.

1961 Freedom Riders protest segregated buses in Deep South.

1962 James Meredith integrates the University of Mississippi.

1963 Civil rights protests explode in Birmingham, Alabama. More than 250,000 Americans participate in March on Washington.

1964 Congress passes Civil Rights Act.

1965 King leads protesters on a march from Selma to Montgomery to press for voting rights. Congress passes Voting Rights Act. Malcolm X assassinated in New York.

1966 Student Non-violent Coordinating Committee (SNCC) splits with SCLC; adopts "black power" slogan. Black Panther Party organized.

1967 Thurgood Marshall named associate justice of U.S. Supreme Court.

1968 Martin Luther King assassinated in Memphis.

1972 New York Congresswoman Shirley Chisholm runs for the Democratic presidential nomination.

1984 The Rev. Jesse Jackson runs for the Democratic presidential nomination and garners significant black and white support.

1988 Jackson again competes for the Democratic nomination and wins 6.6 million votes.

1989 L. Douglas Wilder wins gubernatorial election in Virginia, becoming first African American elected chief executive of a state.

1992 Carol Moseley Braun becomes the first black woman elected to the U.S. Senate.

1993 Toni Morrison wins the Nobel Prize for Literature

1995 Nation of Islam leader Louis Farrakhan leads Million Man March in Washington, D.C.

1997 President Bill Clinton announces his Initiative on Race, and appoints an advisory board chaired by the historian John Hope Franklin to report on the state of race relations in the United States.

Further Reading

Narrative Overviews and Reference Works

Bennett, Lerone, *Before the Mayflower: A History of Black America*, Penguin, 1993.

Blassingame, John, *The Slave Community: Plantation Life in the Antebellum South*, Oxford University Press, 1979.

Franklin, John Hope, and Alfred A. Moss, Jr., *From Slavery to Freedom: A History of African Americans* (7th ed.), McGraw-Hill, 1994.

Harding, Vincent, *There Is a River:The Black Struggle for Freedom in America*, Harcourt Brace, 1981.

Jones, Jacqueline, *Labor of Love, Labor of Sorrow: Black Women, Work and Family, From Slavery to the Present*, Vintage, 1986.

Palmer, Colin A., *Passageways: An Interpretive History of Black America* (2 vols.), Holt, Rinehart & Winston, 1998.

Part I: The Roots of Black America

Blackburn, Robin, *The Making of New World Slavery: From the Baroque to the Modern, 1492–1800*, Verso, 1998.

Brown, Kathleen M., *Good Wives, Nasty Wenches, and Anxious Patriarchs: Gender, Race, and Power in Colonial Virginia*, University of North Carolina Press, 1996.

Curtin, Philip D., *The Atlantic Slave Trade: A Census*, University of Wisconsin Press, 1969.

Jordan, Winthrop D., *White Over Black: American Attitudes Towards the Negro, 1550–1812*, University of North Carolina Press, 1968.

Kolchin, Peter, *American Slavery, 1619–1877*, Hill and Wang, 1993.

Morgan, Edmund, *American Slavery/American Freedom*, W.W. Norton and Co., 1975.

Thomas, Hugh, *The Slave Trade: The Story of the Atlantic Slave Trade, 1440–1870*, Simon and Schuster, 1997.

Thornton, John, *Africa and Africans in the Making of the Modern World, 1400–1800* (2d ed.), Cambridge University Press, 1992.

Wood, Peter, *Black Majority: Negroes in Colonial South Carolina from 1670 through the Stono Rebellion*, W.W. Norton and Co., 1974.

Part II: Two Communities, Slave and Free

Aptheker, Herbert, *American Negro Slave Revolts* (6th ed.), International Publishers, 1993.

Berlin, Ira, *Many Thousands Gone: The First Two Centuries of Slavery in North America*, Belknap Press, 1998.

Campbell, James T., *Songs of Zion: The African Methodist Episcopal Church in the United States and South Africa*, University of North Carolina Press, 1995.

Fox-Genovese, Elizabeth, *Within the Plantation Household: Black and White Women of the Old South*, University of North Carolina Press, 1988.

Genovese, Eugene, *Roll, Jordan, Roll: The World the Slaves Made*, Vintage Books, 1972.

Gutman, Herbert, *The Black Family in Slavery and Freedom, 1750–1825*, Random House, 1976.

Horton, James O., *Free People of Color: Inside the African American Community*, 1993

Litwack, Leon F., *North of Slavery: The Negro in the Free States, 1790–1860*, University of Chicago Press, 1961.

Raboteau, Albert J., *Slave Religion: The Invisible Institution in the Antebellum South*, Oxford University Press, 1980.

Voelz, Peter M., *Slave and Soldier: The Military Impact of Blacks in the Colonial Americas*, Garland, 1993.

Part III: Toward Freedom

DuBois, W. E. B., *Black Reconstruction in America*, Maxwell Macmillan International, 1992.

Fehrenbacher, Don E., *Slavery, Law, and Politics: The Dred Scott Case in Historical Perspective*, Oxford University Press, 1981.

Filler, Louis, *Crusade Against Slavery, 1830–1860*, Reference Publications, 1986.

Foner, Eric, *Reconstruction: America's Unfinished Revolution, 1863–1877*, Harper and Row, 1988.

Freehling, William W., *The Road to Disunion: Secessionists at Bay, 1776–1854*, Oxford University Press, 1990.

Gara, Larry, *The Liberty Line: The Legend of the Underground Railroad*, University of Kentucky Press, 1961.

Levine, Lawrence, *Black Culture and Black Consciousness: Afro-American Folk Thought from Slavery to Freedom*, Oxford University Press, 1978.

McPherson, James M., *Battle Cry of Freedom: The Civil War Era*, Oxford University Press, 1988.

Painter, Nell I., *Exodusters: Black Migration to Kansas After Reconstruction*, Alfred A. Knopf, 1977

Quarles, Benjamin, *Black Abolitionists*, Da Capo Press, 1991.

Stampp, Kenneth M., *The Peculiar Institution: Slavery in the Ante-Bellum South*, Vintage Books, 1989.

Part IV: African Americans Under Arms

Aptheker, Herbert, *The Negro in the Civil War*, International Publishers, 1962.

Berlin, Ira, Joseph P. Reidy, and Leslie S. Rowland, eds., *The Black Military Experience*, Cambridge University Press, 1982.

Francis, Charles E., *The Tuskegee Airmen: The Men Who Changed A Nation* (3rd ed.), Branden Publishing, 1993.

McGregor, Morris J., *Integration of the Armed Forces, 1940–1965*, Center for Military History, 1981.

Mullin, Robert W., *Blacks in America's Wars: The Shift in Attitudes from the Revolutionary War to Vietnam*, Monad Press, 1974.

Nalty, Bernard C., *Strength for the Fight: A History of Black Americans in the Military*, Free Press, 1986.

Williams, Charles H., *Negro Soldiers in World War I: The Human Side*, AMS Press, 1970.

Part V: The Struggle for Equality

Branch, Taylor, *Parting the Waters: America in the King Years, 1954–63*, Simon and Schuster, 1988.

Carmichael, Stokely, and Charles Hamilton, *Black Power: The Politics of Liberation in America*, Penguin, 1969.

Carson, Clayborne, *In Struggle: SNCC and the Black Awakening of the 1960s*, Harvard University Press, 1995.

Chafe, William H., *Civilities and Civil Rights: Greensboro, North Carolina, and the Black*

Struggle for Freedom, Oxford University Press, 1981.

Cronon, E. David, *Black Moses: The Story of Marcus Garvey and the Universal Negro Improvement Association* (2d. ed.), University of Wisconsin Press, 1981.

DuBois, W. E. B., *The Souls of Black Folk, Essays and Sketches* (1903), Penguin, 1996.

Gaines, Kevin K., *Uplifting the Race: Black Leadership, Politics, and Culture in the Twentieth Century*, University of North Carolina Press, 1996.

Garrow, David J., *Bearing the Cross: Martin Luther King, Jr., and the Southern Christian Leadership Conference*, Vintage, 1993.

Haley, Alex, *The Autobiography of Malcolm X*, Ballantine Books, 1965.

Harrison, Alferdteen, ed., *Black Exodus: The Great Migration from the American South*, University Press of Mississippi, 1991.

Lawson, Steven F., *Black Ballots: Voting Rights in the South, 1944–1969*, Columbia University Press, 1976.

Lewis, David Levering, *The Race to Fashoda: European Colonialism and African Resistance to the Scramble for Africa*, Bloomsbury, 1988.

_____, *W. E. B. DuBois: Biography of a Race*, Henry Holt, 1994.

Peterson, Robert, *Only the Ball Was White: A History of Legendary Black Players and All-Black Professional Teams*, Oxford University Press, 1992.

Swain, Carol M., *Black Faces, Black Interests: The Representation of African Americans in Congress*, Harvard University Press, 1995.

Trotter, Joe William, ed., *The Great Migration in Historical Perspective: The Making of an Industrial Proletariat, 1915–45*, Indiana

University Press, 1991.

Woodward, C. Vann, *Origins of the New South*, Louisiana State University Press, 1951.

_____, *The Strange Career of Jim Crow*, Oxford University Press, 1982.

Part VI: The African American Community

Bruce, Dickson, *Black American Writing from the Nadir: The Evolution of a Literary Tradition, 1877–1915*, Louisiana State University Press, 1989.

Huggins, Nathan I., *Harlem Renaissance*, Oxford University Press, 1973.

Lewis, David Levering, *When Harlem Was in Vogue*, Oxford University Press, 1989.

Raboteau, Albert, *A Fire in the Bones: Reflections on African American Religious History*, Beacon Press, 1995.

Sitkoff, Harvard, *A New Deal for Blacks: The Emergence of Civil Rights as an Issue*, Oxford University Press, 1981.

Southern, Eileen, *The Music of Black Americans: A History* (3rd ed.), Norton, 1997.

Stuckey, Sterling, *Going Through the Storm: The Influence of African American Art in History*, Oxford University Press, 1994.

Weiss, Nancy J., *Farewell to the Party of Lincoln: Black Politics in the Age of FDR*, Princeton University Press, 1983.

Woodson, Carter G., *The History of the Negro Church* (3rd ed.), Associated Publishers, 1992.

Index

Acknowledgments

The author wishes to thank the University of Kansas, the Huntington Library, the National Endowment for the Humanities and the American Council of Learned Societies for supporting this project, and Leslie Tuttle, Andrew Frank, and Eric T. L. Love for their suggestions on how to make it better.

Pictures are reproduced by permission of, or have been provided by the following:

American Antiquarian Society: 22
Arcadia Editions Limited: 21, 48
Archive Pictures Inc.: 105
Associated Press Worldwide: 92
Bettmann Archive: 66, 116, 119
Brown Brothers: 96
Brown University: 74
Culver Pictures: 84
e.t. archives: 24, 32
Frank Leslie's Illustrated Newspaper archive: 58
Historic New Orleans Collection: 46
Hulton Getty: 114
Kansas State Historical Society: 69
Library Company of Philadelphia: 44
Library of Congress: 70
Link Picture Library, London: 130
Montana Historical Society: 78
National Archives: 11, 12, 82
Peter Newarks American Pictures: 53, 63, 112, 139
Rockefeller Folk Art Museum: 30
U.S. Army Archives: 90
Private collections

Design: Malcolm Swanston, Elsa Gibert

Cartography: Elsa Gibert, Malcolm Swanston

Drawing p. 21, 48: Peter A. B. Smith.